Q Tasks

*How to empower students to ask questions
and care about answers*

CAROL KOECHLIN

SANDI ZWAAN

Pembroke Publishers Limited

© 2006 Pembroke Publishers
538 Hood Road
Markham, Ontario, Canada L3R 3K9
www.pembrokepublishers.com

Distributed in the U.S. by Stenhouse Publishers
480 Congress Street
Portland, ME 04101-3400
www.stenhouse.com

We acknowledge the financial support of the Government of Canada through the
Book Publishing Industry Development Program (BPIDP) for our publishing
activities.

We acknowledge the assistance of the OMDC Book Fund, an initiative of the Ontario
Media Development Corporation.

Library and Archives Canada Cataloguing in Publication

Koechlin, Carol
    Q tasks : how to empower students to ask questions and care
about answers / Carol Koechlin and Sandi Zwaan.

Includes bibliographical references and index.
ISBN 1-55138-197-4

1. Critical thinking—Study and teaching (Elementary)
2. Creative thinking—Study and teaching (Elementary) I. Zwaan, Sandi
II. Title.

LB1027.44.K64 2006   372.13   C2005-907192-3

Editor: Kat Mototsune
Cover design: John Zehethofer
Typesetting: JayTee Graphics

Printed and bound in Canada
9 8 7 6 5 4

Contents

Introduction

> What an important task we have…to create learning that compels our students past twilight, imbued with a feeling of investigating something enormous! (Debbie Abilock, *Knowledge Quest*)

This imaginative definition of the important work of educators eloquently expresses what we hope readers will feel as they explore this book.

Teaching and learning are so exciting, but ever so complex. For this reason alone we will attempt to keep it simple. We all want our students to be successful. We can measure success with a sigh of satisfaction when we realize, *They got it, they understand*. Having said that, we all know that there is nothing simple about the ability of the human mind to acquire and demonstrate understanding of skills, knowledge, and ideas. Fortunately there are many scholarly studies and resources available to assist us in working out our own personal understanding of what student understanding looks, sounds, and feels like. Individual teachers will build and rebuild their own schema over and over as their experiences build and new challenges unfold.

You understand it only if you can teach it, use it, prove it, explain it, or read between the lines.

(Wiggins and McTighe, *Understanding by Design*)

> The more we understand the brain the better we'll be able to design instruction to match how it learns best … certain activities and strategies are more effective than others in increasing student understanding. (Patricia Wolfe, *Brain Matters*)

One point all the academic experts would agree on is that understanding is a process, not a destination point. With this in mind, we suggest that the most critical key to understanding is the question. Without an inquiry catalyst, student learning would be forever stuck in memorization-and-recall gear. It is the question that stirs the intellect, wakes up the neurons, and provides the stimulus for students to do something with the raw numbers, facts, and data they have gathered or been presented with. The question can be prompted by both the curiosity of the student and the instructional intent of the educator. Both these sources of questions are necessary if students are to learn and ultimately reach real understanding of topics and issues.

The Question Is the Answer to Understanding

Questioning is often thought to be an innate skill, right up there with eating and walking. If you think about it, though, eating and walking are nurtured skills. So it is with questioning.

In spite of the fact that our wee kindergarten students arrive at school bursting with "why?" and "how come?" questions, by the time they are in middle school many have lost this delightful and valuable curiosity. They are so used to answering teacher questions, worrying about marks, and giving the "right" or expected answer that they are stuck in answer gear. How can understanding ever be achieved in this atmosphere? It is not surprising that some students in the middle years become very jaded about school and feel it has no relevance for them. They are tired of answering "fake" questions, those generated by the need to cover curriculum content.

We are not saying that teachers should not develop questions for students to answer. These questions are a necessary component of teaching students how and when to question. What we are saying is this: just try letting go; put the spoon in a student's hand and see what happens. It is not so difficult to turn the tables and teach students how to develop real questions, those that uncover personal understanding for them. Allowing students the exhilaration of learning in an environment where their questions are valued and celebrated will reap rich rewards. When students have some ownership of their learning experience, you will find that enthusiasm, effort, and efficacy will be generated.

Motivation is part of our rationale for teaching students to question. Our main objective is the chemistry that takes place between questions and understanding. The number one reason that many research projects in classrooms are ho-hum bristol board displays or plagiarized reports is because they are driven by the "all about" syndrome. But this is very easy to fix! If you really want your students to demonstrate their personal growth and understanding through assigned research projects, then they must process the data they have gathered through the lens of a good inquiry question or challenge.

Once you have learned how to ask relevant and appropriate questions, you have learned how to learn and no one can keep you from learning whatever you want or need to know.

(Neil Postman and Charles Weingartner, *Teaching as a Subversive Activity*)

"The mere formulation of a problem is far more essential than its solution, which may be merely a matter of mathematical or experimental skills. To raise new questions, new possibilities, to regard old problems from a new angle requires creative imagination and marks real advances in science."
Albert Einstein

Students cannot be expected to think critically and creatively about the ideas and knowledge of others unless they possess that magical chemical ingredient—the question—to kickstart the process. The question can take the form of an inquiry question or statement. It can be a challenge, problem to solve, or decision to make; but it must be there or the assignment becomes an exercise in pretend research. We all know the result—cut, paste, and plagiarize!

The information available to students today renders it impossible to approach learning without questioning skills. The vast volumes of data available today on any given topic can be managed and analyzed only by people who are information literate. Educating students for the 21st century requires that educators teach students how to be critical and creative users of information. Neither attribute—being critical or creative—can be accomplished unless students are also effective questioners.

Silent-Head Questions

Questioning also plays a huge role in learning to learn. This kind of questioning is not as easy to define as the research question. These are questions that are often not voiced, but are mumbled inside our heads as we proceed with a task. Making students aware of these inner mumblings will help them develop metacognitive abilities.

To nurture learning, it is necessary for students to question so that they have better strategies for interacting with text; it is the question that allows students to make the important self-to-text relationship. Without the silent-head question, analysis of data and ideas would not take place. We can model these questions for students in think-alouds, showing them how we question in our heads as we read a newspaper article, analyze a bill from the hydro company, or examine an art object.

Help students become conscious of these silent-head questions, and control the quality of their quests by having them write down questions until the process becomes intuitive. We offer several tasks in this book to help with this strategy.

> Without strong questioning skills, you are just a passenger on someone else's tour bus. You may be on the highway, but someone else is doing the driving. (Jamie McKenzie, *Learning to Question to Wonder to Learn*)

Questioning skills will also equip students with the tools to self-analyze. It is with self-questioning that we assess our results and our effort, as well as setting goals for improvement. Again, you need to model how this works and give students ample opportunities to "drive their own bus."

It is our belief that questioning is at the very core of understanding. Every nugget of learning germinates from an investigation of some kind.

Questioning needs to be nurtured and developed at all ages and for all disciplines.

Questioning is an essential skill.

Questioning is the answer to understanding.

How Do We Nurture the Process of Inquiry?

Increase learning and student achievement by elevating the level of investigation.

Curriculum Focus – Identify what it is you want students to know and be able to do, as well as how students will demonstrate their understanding.

Rich Information – Gather the best resources available to support learning. Consider variety, readability, balanced perspectives, and accessibility.

Engaging Thinking – Design experiences with these rich resources for students to explore the topic and look for connections. These activities should spark their curiosity and wonderment about the topic, as well as building background information.

Building the Question(s) – Ensure that students own the question(s). Provide opportunities and tools to help students design lots of questions until they find the "just right" question for them and/or their specific information need.

Deep Thinking – As students work with information, the guiding question(s) will keep them on track and kickstart critical and analytical thinking about the data they collect. This kind of analysis elevates thinking beyond just gathering and recording, cutting and pasting.

Deeper Understanding – Answering the question will ensure that students reach levels of synthesis. They will draw conclusions, solve problems, make decisions, and invent and create new meaning for themselves when their thinking is driven by their question. Deeper thinking based on effective questions eliminates the possibility of plagiarized reports!

So What? – Students must have opportunities to share their learning authentically with others in order to further value and understand the significance of their findings. They must have opportunities to transfer and apply their learning, to reach metacognition.

The cycle continues as students formulate new questions and/or decide to take action.

Using this Book

We trust that the title of this book, *Q Tasks: How to empower students to ask questions and care about answers,* will help readers understand that this book is not about teacher-directed questions in the classroom. It is, in fact, about turning the tables and empowering students to develop questions themselves. Modeling good questions is an important part of the learning process, and we have woven this important step into the tasks we have developed. There are many professional texts devoted to the teacher as questioner; we saw a need for more practical support for the student as questioner.

> Our hope is that the ideas presented in this book will be a starting point for teachers.

Our goal is to help students build a repertoire of effect strategies and learn to create questions for all kinds of tasks:

- connecting with literature and the arts
- exploring scientific and mathematical concepts
- delving deeper into world issues
- self-analysis and goal setting
- problem solving real-world as well as personal queries
- guiding research quests
- evaluating the reliability of information
- testing new ideas
- inventing
- and more…

The mercuric nature of questioning made our job as authors very tricky. Questioning is not like other skills in the curriculum, for which set rules and processes apply. Effective questioning relies on the inner thoughts, experiences, specific needs, and emotions of the questioner. Questioning is just as much spontaneous and reactionary as it is thoughtful and planned. Having said that, we firmly believe that effective questioning can be taught and practised. If we are to fully prepare students to participate and thrive at learning, working, and playing in the 21st century, we must equip them with questioning know-how.

In organizing the Q Tasks, we have attempted to analyze the nebulous structure of the question. We have arranged our strategies to create a continuum of approaches. We hope our readers will be able to work with this structure and adapt it to fit their own needs, as they go about building a culture of inquiry in their classrooms, libraries, schools, and communities.

The Q Tasks are organized in five chapters.

Chapter 1 Encouraging Curiosity
This section builds on innate human nature and provides points for nurturing curiosity and cultivating wonder and imagination.

Chapter 2 Understanding Questions

The question comes under the microscope and is analyzed for structure and purpose.

Chapter 3 Learning to Question

Collections of tried and true processes for building good questions are shared.

Chapter 4 Questioning to Learn

Many applications for questioning in multiple disciplines, age groups, and abilities are presented.

Chapter 5 Questioning to Progress

These tasks provide transference for students, allowing them to be able to self-question and apply their questioning skills for continuous growth.

Chapter 6 Moving Forward

This chapter will bring our readers full circle, back to the introduction and the importance of questions in building understanding. This is not a final chapter but the beginning of a quest for teachers.

Within each chapter, the Q Tasks have been developed to teach the specific skills and attributes that effective questioners need. The order of the tasks is not intended to be rigid, but simply demonstrates a possible skill-building approach. Classroom teachers and teacher-librarians will need to design a continuum that works for their own student needs.

Each Q Task addresses a teacher need in the form of a question. The "Q Task" description appears on the notepad at the left in student outcome language. Curriculum context for the task is explained in "Clarifying the Task." Teaching and learning strategies for the lesson are outlined in "Building Understanding." What students will be asked to do to show that they can use the skill, as well as other assessment tips, are in the section called "Demonstrating Understanding." The "Q Tip" offers further resources or extensions.

Within each chapter there are also one or more pages of Q Task Quickies. These are usually extensions to a skill already introduced.

We hope we have been successful in lassoing and tying down our questioning ideas and melding them with the excellent work of others before us.

1. Encouraging Curiosity

How can we harness the power of curiosity as a catalyst for learning?

Curiosity and questioning go hand-in-hand in the development of higher-level thinking skills and teaching for understanding. Curiosity fuels imagination and leads to wonderment; thus it is a prerequisite to good questioning. Engagement is sparked by curiosity, then deep thinking is guided by the question. So curiosity is a critical factor in the learning process, both as a motivator and a facilitator.

To engage this natural energy we must surround students with a rich learning environment—access to a school library, well-stocked with resources and rich with programs. Borrow bushels of books from the school library to build your rotating classroom libraries. Make sure that classroom collections are always fresh and stimulating. Use these excellent resources as springboards to wonder and imagination about other people, places, events, places, times, and feelings. Link students to even more experiences vicariously through selected web sites, good educational videos, virtual museums, and archives. In today's information glut, it is of paramount importance to ensure that students have access to the best sources of information. Work toward providing 24/7 virtual access to rich resources and support through thoughtfully crafted school library web pages. Provide real-time access to information experts through guest speakers, performances, field trips, and interactive video conferencing experiences.

To stimulate curiosity, provide lots of hands-on and minds-on (Wiggins and McTighe, 1998) learning experiences in all subject areas and for all ages. Although questioning is a valued component in most well-designed process approaches to learning, it is not often that student questioning is guiding the process.

Young children seem to have endless questions about their environment; in later school years there is little evidence of this innate ability to question. If we can rekindle this natural interest and wonderment, then students are likely to take a more active role in their learning and to sense a greater relevance. How can we do this?

First we want to develop an awareness of their "curiosity quotient" and how it factors into their learning success. Then we must encourage enthusiasm for the art of questioning. We need to create an environment where asking questions is recognized as part of the learning process, where it is applauded, where it is encouraged and spontaneous.

To help do this, we have revisited some of the games that children have played, over the decades, with great enthusiasm. We will also utilize the power of excellent picture books as a catalyst for building wonder and curiosity.

The tasks that follow are designed to help spark and develop more curious students.

- What are the benefits of curiosity?
- How does curiosity empower students as questioners?
- How can we use 20 Questions?
- Q Task Quickies: Variations on 20 Questions
- How can riddles engage reluctant readers?
- How can I help students create riddles?
- Q Task Quickies: More Riddles
- Q Task Quickies: Question Quiver
- How can I arouse students' curiosity about a new curriculum topic?
- Q Task Quickies: Building Wonder

> "The whole art of teaching is only the art of awakening the natural curiosity of young minds for the purpose of satisfying it afterwards."
>
> Anatole France

What are the benefits of curiosity?

Q Task
Students will reflect on their own curiosity and how it empowers their learning potential.

Clarifying the Task

Curiosity is an important factor in the learning process, both as a motivator and a facilitator. In this task, students will consider some well-known quotations to help them develop a personal understanding of curiosity, allowing you to tap into their natural curiosity to get them hooked on the subject and engaged in the activity.

Building Understanding

- Select a quote to model this task; for example, "We keep moving forward, opening new doors, and doing new things, because we are curious and curiosity keeps leading us down new paths" (Walt Disney). See Curiosity Quotes for more. Ask students what they think the quotation means. Discuss how the quotation might inspire them to be more curious. Chart responses.
- Divide the class into groups and provide each group with one curiosity quote in the centre of a large piece of chart paper. Allow time for the group to discuss the quote and "graffiti" their reactions on the chart paper around the quote. Have groups rotate to visit each quote and add additional responses to the graffiti. Post the charts around the room.

Curiosity Quotes

- "Curiosity killed the cat." (Unknown)
- "Curiosity did not kill the cat. This is a silly myth. A dangerous message." (Jamie McKenzie)
- "The cure for boredom is curiosity. There is no cure for curiosity." (Dorothy Parker)
- "Curiosity is one of the permanent and certain characteristics of a vigorous mind." (Samuel Johnson)
- "I have no special talents. I am only passionately curious." (Albert Einstein)

Demonstrating Understanding

Use question prompts to help students make links between curiosity and learning:

- Which subjects are you most interested in? What is it about these subjects that interests you?
- Are there certain topics within these subjects that hold more interest than others? Which? Why?
- If you could study/investigate anything you wanted to, what would it be?
- How does your curiosity about a topic affect how you approach it, how hard you work at it, how much you remember?

Debrief and allow students time to write a reflection for their learning log by selecting one of the quotes and relating how that quote is reflective of their beliefs about curiosity.

Q Tip
I still remember an English classroom at college with a sign over the door stating, "A love of literature is caught, not taught." While I don't recall the master's name, I do remember his passion for literature and I did catch the bug. I was immediately intrigued, curious about how to facilitate the "catching." Was I more receptive to the enthusiasm he exuded because my curiosity was tweaked by the sign?

How does curiosity empower students as questioners?

Q Task
Students will begin to understand the connections between curiosity and questioning.

Clarifying the Task
Welcoming and encouraging natural curiosity is a first step in building a culture of inquiry. In this task, students will explore curious characters in a story, and then examine their own curiosity quotient.

Building Understanding
- Introduce this activity by reading and discussing a story that has an overtly curious character; e.g., *The Pigeon Finds a Hot Dog* by Mo Willems.
- Ask students to define curiosity, then ask them to show evidence that the duck in this story is in fact the curious bird as he claims to be.
- Have students brainstorm for other characters in books, film, or television that have a high degree of curiosity.
- Provide students with the How Curious Are You? organizer (page 15). Read the questions together and ask students to answer this self-survey as honestly as they can. Explain that you are not looking for right or wrong answers. The purpose of the survey is to help everyone gain confidence and understand the connections between curiosity and becoming a good questioner.
- Discuss with students any thoughts and concerns they are comfortable sharing after completing the survey.

Demonstrating Understanding
❏ Provide students with the My Point of View organizer (page 16).
❏ Instruct students to think about the story you explored, and to reflect on their survey and discussions about curiosity.
❏ Ask students to think about the positives and negatives of curiosity and complete the organizer using the prompts to help them form a point of view.

Q Tip
Curiosity is a valued trait for inventors, artists, and entrepreneurs. This task could be an excellent prelude to study of famous people, inventions, or artistic experimentation.

How Curious Are You?

Do you ever ask questions in class?

When is it easy to ask questions at school or at home?

When is it difficult or uncomfortable to ask questions?

Do you like it when other students ask questions?

How do other students' questions help you learn?

How do your teachers' questions help you?

How do your own questions help you?

What do you think curiosity is?

Do you know a very curious person? Share some examples of their curiosity.

My Point of View

That's Good	Why?					That's Bad	Why?				

I think that...

On the other hand,...

My personal view is...

How can we use 20 Questions?

Q Task

Students will apply strategic questioning skills in the game format called 20 Questions.

Clarifying the Task

This is an excellent strategy for developing the strategic application of questioning skills. It is an engaging activity to review course content. In this task example, the class has just finished a unit on the classification of animals.

Building Understanding

- Group students in teams of five. Assign one student in each group to select the animal that the other four students will work together to identify with their questions.
- The questioners can ask only questions to which the answer is "Yes" or "No"; the total number of questions they can ask is 20.
- The student who selected the topic will keep track of the questions or assign one student to be the record keeper and timer (if you want to set a time limit to move the questioning along).
- At any time a team questioner may ask, "Is it…?" If the guess is incorrect, the game continues. You can set a limit to the number of direct guesses that can be asked in any round.
- The object is to question strategically so as not to waste questions, and for students to build on each others' questions.
- As each animal is identified, a new student decides on the next topic to be guessed and the process continues until all students have had a turn or until time for the activity expires.
- As with all new strategies, model this with the entire class first and keep practising until students have the skills to work in small groups.

Demonstrating Understanding

Debrief the activity with the students and list the strategies they thought worked well, and some of the problems they had. Ask them to reflect on the game process and to complete the My Thoughts About 20 Questions learning log (page 18), so they can learn to articulate how their teams used strategic thinking and good questioning skills to guess their animal.

Q Tip

Use 20 Questions at all age levels for review of historical figures and events, geographic locations, children's authors, popular cultural figures, and science topics. It is a wonderful activity for rainy-day recess or long bus trips.

My Thoughts About 20 Questions

How did the 20 Questions game help you to review our topic today? Why?

What was difficult about this activity?

What strategies did you and your team use to guess the topic?

How well did your team work together?

What would you like your team to do next time you play 20 questions?

Variations on 20 Questions

The Question Box

- Decorate a medium-sized box with a lid. Inside the box place an item you want your students to discover. The item could have a specific purpose for your program or be an interest item, such as a signed baseball. It could relate to a theme or content unit you want to introduce; e.g., a popular book to introduce teen reading week, a lunchbox to introduce a unit on nutrition. Younger students could bring in their treasures as a diversion from traditional Show and Tell.
- The exercise should take no more than three to five minutes. Making it a timed item will encourage more participation. The class can ask Yes or No questions, but they have only 20 altogether.
- The purpose is to practise questioning skills and strategically build on the questions of others in order for the class to deduce the answer to "What is in the question box today?"

I'm thinking of… What is it?

This old game, usually played on long car trips, is another great strategy for practising purposeful questioning techniques. One student thinks of something for the others to guess and provides clues.

> - *I am thinking of something that is green.* **What is it?**
> - *I am thinking of something that begins with the letter "K."* **What is it?**
> - *I am thinking of an animal that lives on the farm.* **What is it?**

The class then has 20 questions to guess the answer.

Picture Quest

For those who like to sketch
- Each student makes a sketch of something they are interested in; e.g., sports equipment or icon, road sign, logo. etc. The sketch could also be more specific, like something that gives a clue to a book or song title.
- Instruct students to fold their sketches and place each in an envelope.
- Group students in triads.
- One student per triad opens their envelope and shares their sketch. The other two students take turns asking questions, using the 20-questions technique, to determine what each sketch represents.
- Move to the next student in the triad and resume 20 questions until all three sketches have been identified.

How can riddles engage reluctant readers?

Clarifying the Task

Riddles are quite a sophisticated form of questioning, requiring complex thought and problem-solving skills to both create and answer. Riddles are also engaging for reluctant readers. Often riddles can be linked to popular media characters, giving students an opportunity to make connections with personal knowledge and experiences. Riddles can also be an engaging way to share or review newly acquired facts in content subjects.

Building Understanding

Introduce the Q Task with a group circle sharing. Read a few riddles from your favorite book, such as the award-winning *Ha Ha Ha* by Lyn Thomas. Invite students to share their favorite riddles, in turn, around the circle. (To ensure that all students are prepared to participate, the previous day assign the creation of a riddle for homework and have them bring it in for sharing.) When sharing is completed ask students if any of the riddles they heard sounded similar. Did they hear any repeated patterns for riddles? Create a Riddle Patterns chart of their ideas and discuss their discoveries.

Demonstrating Understanding

❏ Form small teams of three or four students. Provide each group with a recording sheet, some sticky notes, and a good selection of riddle books. Each group will need four to five books. (Supplement the school classroom and library collection of riddle books with copies borrowed from your local public library, as well as favorites brought to class by the students)

❏ Invite students to read, share, and examine the riddle books, looking for similarities and patterns in the riddles.

❏ Have students attach sticky notes to pages, and record the pages and books where they found riddles with similar patterns.

❏ Have the group keep a record of the similarities and patterns they find and be prepared to share their discoveries:

- "Knock, knock"
- "Who/what am I?"
- "How many _____ does it take to change a light bulb?"
- "Why did the _____ cross the road?"
- "How do you know…?"
- "What do you get when….?"
- "What did one_____ say to…?"

Q Tip

Web sites are also a rich source of riddles.

- *Not so hard Riddles*
  http://www.niehs.nih.gov/kids/rd1.htm
- *Insect Riddles*
  http://www.k12.de.us/lfeast/lessons/insect/insect3.htm
- *Riddle Interactive*
  http://www.readwritethink.org/materials/riddle/index.html
- *Just Riddles and More*
  http://www.justriddlesandmore.com/kidsriddles.html

How can I help students create riddles?

Q Task
Students will apply riddle questioning patterns and word associations to create their own riddles.

Clarifying the Task
Students are now familiar with riddle patterns and questions. They will learn how to apply this knowledge to create their own original riddles that are based on familiar texts and concepts such as fairy tales, classic stories, and nursery rhymes.

Building Understanding
- Review similarities and patterns found in riddles in the Q Task on page 20.
- Read a familiar story such as *The Shoemaker and the Elves*. Ask students to list characters and objects from the story. Using the Just Like organizer (page 21), have students select objects or characters and brainstorm connections. Students could also create a web about the story to expand their thinking about possible connections.
- Revisit the Riddle Patterns chart (see page 20) and give students some time to think of a riddle based on the story. Share and chart the riddles.
- Re-read the story in another version; if possible show a video adaptation. Again give students some think time to compose their new riddles. Share and chart.

This is a good time to establish some class guidelines regarding acceptable riddle content. Discuss the difference between clever riddles and those that are mean or rude.

Demonstrating Understanding
Have students search for a fairy tale or classic story they would like to compose riddles about. Remind students to prepare by making a web or using the Just Like organizer. A dictionary and thesaurus could also be useful for expanding ideas. Encourage them to refer to the class chart of Riddle Patterns for ideas to get started. Have students test out their riddles with other students and revise as necessary.

Q Tip
- Riddles could be assembled into a class book, displayed around the school, or published in newsletters and on the school web site.
- A collection of homonyms can be very useful for creating riddles.

Just Like

Word/Character	Looks Like	Sounds Like	Tastes/Smells Like	Feels like

More Riddles

For these versions of the riddle tasks, instruct students to recall important information from your focus topic and jot down the key facts. Now have them turn the facts around to formulate trivia-type questions that have short-phrase or one-word answers. *Who, what, when, where,* and sometimes *how* are usually the best question starters for this task.

Students share their riddle-type questions in a creative format. Have students trade and solve each other's questions. These tasks are engaging ways to build language skills and to consolidate and review course content for all ages and curricula.

Crosswords

Commercial software and web-based crossword makers are available. They make the creation of a crossword easy once you have the trivia questions and answers.

- http://www.puzzlemaker.com/
- http://www.searchamateur.com/corkboard/Crossword-puzzle.html
- http://www.puzzlemesilly.com/
- http://www.awesomeclipartforkids.com/crossword/crosswordpuzzlemaker.html

Lift-the-Flap Page or Booklet

Instruct students to record trivia questions on medium-sized sticky notes or colored paper shapes. They will fasten one edge of their question flap to the paper and write or sketch the answer to each question under the appropriate flap. There are endless possibilities for format.

Interactive Riddles

Teach students how to use features of commercial slideshow programs such as PowerPoint or Hyperstudio. Hyperlinks, animation, and other special effects have great potential to spark the imaginations of your students as they produce their interactive riddle shows.

Question Quiver

This is an old, time-tested game that students still enjoy. Create Question Quivers, commonly known as Cootie Catchers or Fortune Tellers, using instructions on page 26. Label with numbers and colors as usual, but use the inner flaps, where the answers traditionally go, for questions.

See how many other applications you and your students can find for this strategy.

Book Review

Motivate students to discuss a book they have recently read by using their Question Quivers as a game. Use questions like these:

- Why would someone else like to read this book?
- Who else might like to read this book?
- Which character would you like as a friend/relative? Why?
- What made the plot believable?
- How did the setting affect the story?
- What feelings did you experience as you read the story?
- What did you like best about the book?
- What suggestion do you have for the author?

Group-Work Evaluation

To motivate student reflection after a group-work activity, use Question Quivers with questions about the group work.

- How did group members support each other?
- What helped your group stay on task?
- What could your group do to improve?
- What did your group do best?
- Which group role do you prefer?
- How did your working as a group make this a more valuable experience?
- What did you discover about the talents/skills of group members?
- How did your group make sure everyone could contribute?

Question Quiver (continued)

Pre-reading Activity

You are about to begin a novel study with your class. To stimulate interest and thought about the book, have students quiz each other with Question Quivers.

- Based on the title, what do you think this book is about?
- Judging from the cover illustration, what are you expecting?
- How did the blurb on the back of the book affect your opinion?
- Where do think the book will take place?
- Why do you think the teacher chose this book for the class to read?
- What do you know about the author?
- How does what you know about the author affect your expectation for the book?
- Having seen the cover and read the title and back cover blurb, what are you curious about?

Test Preparation

Once students have had several experiences using teacher-prepared questions for their Question Quivers, have them apply what they have learned to create their own questions. As students are preparing for a unit review test, have them individually create eight quiz questions about the unit for their Question Quivers. Allow time to quiz several other classmates to prepare for the test.

Making a Question Quiver

Here's how to make it:

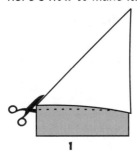 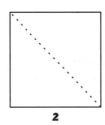 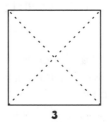 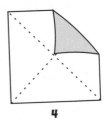

1   2   3   4

1. If you start with a standard sheet of paper, you will need to make it square by folding one corner over to the edge and cutting off the extra strip.
2. Unfold it and you have a square. Fold the other opposite corners together and crease again.
3. Unfold so you are back to the square.
4. Next, fold each corner point into the centre of the creases.

 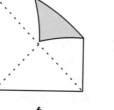 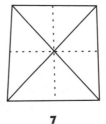 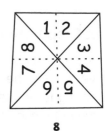

5   6   7   8

5. With all four corners folded, it should look like this.
6. Next, flip it over and fold all four corners points into the centre again.
7. With all of the corners folded in, it will look like this.
8. Write the numbers 1 to 8, with two numbers per flap.

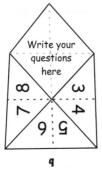  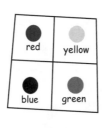 

9   10   11

9. Lift up the flaps and write 8 questions under the numbers.
10. Flip it over and color or write the name of a different color on each of the four flaps.
11. Flip it back over and stick your thumbs and forefingers into the pockets. Fingers should press centre creases so that all four flaps meet at a point in the centre.

How can I arouse students' curiosity about a new curriculum topic?

Q Task
Students will begin to question using *I Wonder* prompts.

Clarifying the Task
The class is finding out about the importance of community workers; e.g., nurse, doctor, teacher, police officer, fire fighter, postal worker. They will become familiar with the language of inquiry and record their own personal wonderings and discoveries.

Building Understanding
Prepare for a guest community worker to visit the classroom. Before the guest arrives, ask students what they wonder about the work this person does. Create a class chart of wonderings. Wonderings can be elicited with prompts such as

- *We wonder if...*
- *We wonder when...*
- *We wonder how..., etc.*

Refer to this chart to focus learning during the visit. When the guest leaves, review the session by collectively answering the wonderings and recording the discoveries.

> "He who wonders discovers that this in itself is wonder."
> M.C. Escher

Demonstrating Understanding
The students will create their own wonderings about a community worker of their choice. Create *I Wonder* booklets for students to record their "I wonder..." questions and research findings. Provide students with several resources at their reading level so they will be able to find the answers to their wonderings. Students who have low language skills may need a learning buddy to help them read and record. Very young researchers can record with pictures, and learning buddies can scribe for them.

Q Tip
I Wonder booklets can be in the form of folded books, fan books, flipbooks, flap books, tall books, or books of different shapes.
See these resources for simple, easy-to-follow instructions:
- *Let's Book It with Tech'knowledge'y* http://www.vickiblackwell.com/makingbooks/
- *Shining Hours* http://www.shininghours.com/creating/one_sheet_8_pages!.htm
- *The Ultimate Guide to Classroom Publishing* by Judy Green (1999)

Building Wonder

Imagine

Good picture books develop imagination. Many can be used as a catalyst for student writing and illustration.

- *Imagine a Night* and *Imagine a Day* by Rob Gonsalves provide a wonderful framework for patterning. After celebrating these delightful works, ask students to "Imagine a… (Holiday, Family, Time, Town, Summer, etc.)," and to write and illustrate their own Imagine Book. Or they can work collaboratively to create a class book.
- Travel back in time with Aunt Violet as she reminisces about her long life and all the changes she has experienced in Jane Wilson's historical picture book, *Imagine That*. Build wonder with your own students by having them interview an elder and develop their own *Imagine that…, Imagine when…* timeline story.

What If…?

- Have students work in small groups of three or four. Provide each group with a different short story (at their reading level) to read and work with.
- Instruct groups to read the story and then think about alternative endings using the *What if…?* prompt.
- Have students record their *What If…?* ideas, then individually select one and rewrite the ending to the original story.

I Wonder Wheel

Any topic can be explored with the *I Wonder* Wheel (page 30).
- Provide students with background information about the topic of study. Children cannot demonstrate curiosity about a topic they have little or no experience with. Background information can be quickly built by viewing a short video, showing pictures, reading books, listening to a guest speaker, etc.
- Make the *I Wonder* Wheel:
  - Cut out the wheel and glue it to a paper plate.
  - Glue the arrow onto cardboard and cut out.
  - Attach the arrow to the centre of the wheel to create a spinner.

  As an alternative, you can build a larger class wheel.
- Instruct students to spin the dial. The question starter the dial stops at is used to generate an I Wonder question about the topic.

This exercise is designed to explore a topic further by developing questions orally, but students could record their I Wonder questions as well.

Building Wonder (continued)

Scientific Wonder

Have students develop wondering questions before, during, and after working on a science experiment or technology exploration. Model the process for students in a demonstration lesson. Even very young scientists can learn how to record their findings and wonderings on the My Scientific Discoveries organizer (page 31). They may need a learning buddy to help them record their findings.

I Wonder **Wheel**

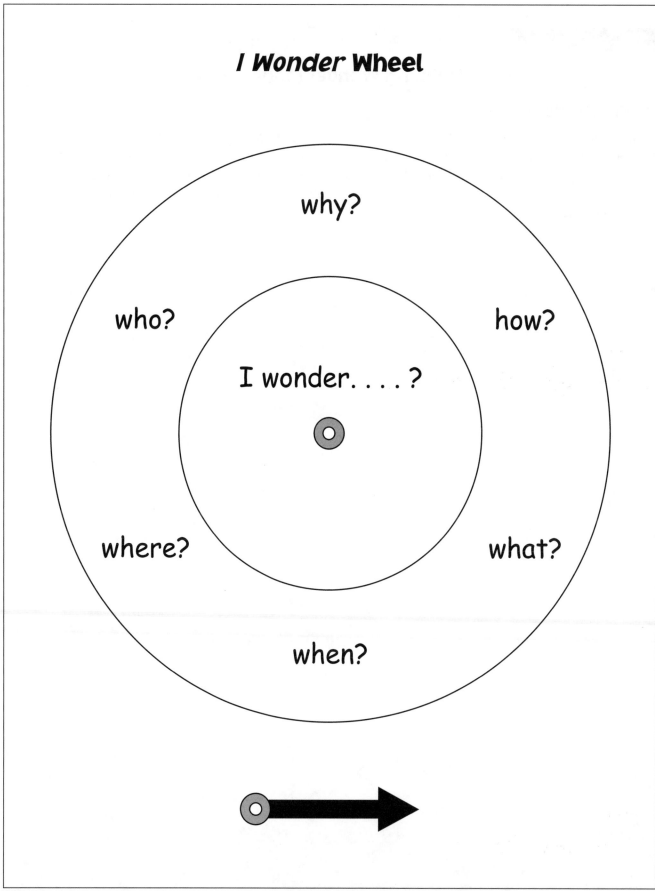

My Scientific Discoveries

I wonder if...

Perhaps...

I tried...

A picture of what happened

I discovered...

Now I wonder why...

2. Understanding Questions

How can we help students develop understanding about questions and questioning?

The Question is the Answer ... Smart questions are essential technology for those who venture on to the Information Highway.

(Jamie McKenzie, 1997)

When we empower students to differentiate between types of questions, they can begin to understand not only how to answer questions but how to create them as well. We want them to think about the purpose of the question and how that affects the construction of the question.

The process of generating questions depends on the ability to identify different cognitive levels of questions (Ciardiello, 1998). This is a complex feat because there are so many types of questions and so many purposes for asking them. It's important to gather lots and lots of question samples and lead students through a process of discovery to help them uncover some patterns for themselves. We build on that experience by introducing and modeling several basic questioning and thinking organizational structures, such as the ReQuest Strategy, deBono's Six Thinking Hats, and Bloom's Taxonomy.

Once students can classify questions they will be able to identify the appropriate action and make an effective plan to source the answers: reading the text independently, making inferences, discussing with peers, or doing some research. The ability to identify the question type and the source of the answer will have a positive affect on reading comprehension of both fiction and non-fiction text types.

The following strategies direct students to consider the question type and look for clues about how and where to seek the answer.

- How can I use Question Hunt?
- How can I help students observe different question types?
- How do I teach open and closed questions?
- How will the ReQuest strategy help students identify question types?
- How can I help students create questions for specific purposes?
- How can coding questions help students look for the answers?
- Q Task Quickies: de Bono's Six Thinking Hats
- What can we learn from famous quotations about questions?

> "If one is master of one thing and understands one thing well, one has at the same time insight into and understanding of many things."
> Vincent van Gogh

How can I use Question Hunt?

Q Task

Students will begin to understand that there is a broad range of questions with different purposes.

Clarifying the Task

This task can be used for students at varying levels of expertise and experience to build background knowledge about questioning. Don't rush this activity. Allow a sufficient period of time for students to build up a rich collection of questions.

Building Understanding

- Introduce this activity by reading and discussing a story about collecting things, such as *If You Find a Rock* by Peggy Christian. Each of the rocks in this story has a different use or purpose, as well as a different structure, but they are all rocks. So it is with questions.
- Inform students that they are going on a question hunt. Provide students with newspapers, magazines, and pamphlets and ask them to look for and clip questions. Students can keep their question collections in an envelope.
- Give students copies of the I Love Questions organizer (page 34) and ask them to maintain a log of questions they hear or read over a period of time. Let them fill up as many organizers as possible; you will need lots and lots of samples.
- Model the next step in the process. Record a dozen or so of the questions on large strips of paper. Post and read the questions and ask students to look for similarities in the questions. Can they think of ways to sort and organize the questions? Organize and reorganize the questions in as many ways as possible, so students can see that questions have different structures and different purposes.

Demonstrating Understanding

❏ Have students cut their I Love Questions sheets into strips and assemble the questions with the ones clipped form newspapers and magazines.

❏ Group students in partners. Provide the students with a large piece of paper and glue sticks.

❏ Instruct each pair to read their questions, look for similarities and differences, and sort their collective questions into categories. Allow them time to move the question strips around on the page as necessary.

❏ Once students are happy with their organization, ask them to glue strips in place and name their categories.

❏ Share results and collectively build a bank of ideas for organizing questions for structure and/or purpose. Fill the walls and halls with We Love Questions.

Q Tip

Possible criteria for sorting:

- Starter word: *who, what, when, where, why, how, if, should, could,* etc.
- Common verb: *is, are, was, were, did, does, can, could, might,* etc.
- To find out feelings, time, place, events, facts, people, opinion, etc.
- Complexity: simple facts, requires research, decision making, open-ended, etc.

I ♥ Questions

_____

_____

_____

_____

_____

_____

_____

How can I help students observe different question types?

Clarifying Understanding

Questions do follow some basic rules. Allow students to look for patterns and build their own understanding through analysis of a variety of sample question types and formats.

Building Understanding

- Have students work in groups using the Close-Up Look at Questions organizer (page 36).
- Provide students with text from a novel that has lots of questions in it. Ask one student to read the text aloud.
- Have students look for similarities and differences in the questions and record their findings on the organizer, using the headings Looks Like, Sounds Like, and Uses of Questions.

They should be able to make some general observations like the following:

- Usually begins with *who, what, when, where, why,* and *how.*
- Can also begin with a verb, such as *is, are, can, will, do, could, might,* etc.
- Always ends with a question mark.
- Can be just one word: Why? How? When? Who? Where?
- Can be open or closed.
- Always makes us think.
- Voice usually rises at the end.

- Select video news clips, interviews, or dramatic productions that overtly model different styles of questions. Have students watch and listen to them, observing body language and listening to voice changes as the people in the clips ask questions. Have students add these observations to their lists.
- Now ask students when and why we use questions. Have students list the uses of questions on their organizer. Share and build a class list.

Demonstrating Understanding

Have students work in their groups to build a web about questions, incorporating everything they know about questions.

Q Tip

Archives for primary source video and sound clips:
- http://archives.cbc.ca
- http://www.cnn.com/video/

Close-Up Look at Questions

Looks Like	Sounds Like

Uses of Questions

How do I teach open and closed questions?

Q Task
Students will classify questions as open or closed.

Clarifying the Task
Helping students discover that there are different kinds of questions with different purposes is the first step to conscientious design of effective questions.

Building Understanding
- Put several items in a box and close the box. Pass it around the class and ask, "What is in the box?"
- Encourage students to use all their senses to guess what might be in the box. Explain to students that, just as the box is closed, so is the question that you asked. The answer to the question can easily be found by opening the box and looking inside. Questions that can easily be answered by looking for facts and figures or by observation are closed questions. These are the kinds of questions teachers ask when they want to know if you can recall information. They are questions that people ask when they need specific information.
- Open the box and show students the items. Ask students the second question: "Which item in the box is the most important?" This is a question that could have many different answers depending on whom you ask. It is an open question because there is no one right or wrong answer.
- Ask students to work in groups to make up lots of questions about the items in the box. Have students classify their questions as open or closed. Which questions are more interesting and why?

Demonstrating Understanding
❏ Provide a chart of five or six questions about a familiar topic.
❏ Using a think-aloud, model for students how you would classify these questions as open or closed. Instruct students to select a dozen or so questions from I Love Questions collection from the Question Hunt Q Task (page 33). Have them classify these questions as open or closed, and record them on the Thinking about Questions organizer (page 38).
❏ Ask students to select one question that they are really curious about and tell why that question is so intriguing for them.

Q Tip
Continue to reinforce this concept with questions in novel studies and content subjects. Occasionally play a quick game with the class when questions are asked: Have the class raise a closed fist if a question is closed and an open palm when questions are open.

Thinking about Questions

Closed	Open

Select one question you are curious about. Explain why you like that question.

How will the ReQuest strategy help students identify question types?

Q Task

Students will understand the ReQuest strategy and identify questions by type.

Clarifying the Task

This task introduces students to another way to classify questions. The ReQuest Procedure (Manzo, 1969) is a structured process of matching need to question type. Using this strategy will help students realize that questions are designed very purposefully based on the intent of the questioner. ReQuest strategy will help students make meaning when they encounter any text.

ReQuest Procedure

On the Line questions: The answers to these questions are found directly in the text (facts already known).

Between the Lines questions: To answer these questions, students select clues from the text. Students need to make some inferences based on information they read. The process of developing questions based on these inferences will also help shape their understanding of the text.

Beyond the Line questions: These questions are usually reflective in nature. The questioner is making connections with the text and other concepts or ideas related to the text. The answers to these questions require thought about the implications of the facts and clues.

Building Understanding

- Select and read aloud a classic picture book or tale, such as "The Hockey Sweater" by Roch Carrier, that the students are already quite familiar with.
- Create On the Line, Between the Lines, and Beyond the Line questions based on the story. Pose these questions to the students and discuss possible answers. Ask the students where or how they would find the answers to these questions.
- Prepare a chart and introduce the three types of questions from the ReQuest Procedure.

Question	Where/how can we find the answer?

- Continue modeling until students seem confident with identifying question types.

Demonstrating Understanding

- ❏ Select several stories and prepare a set of questions for each story with several examples of all three types of questions.
- ❏ Put students in groups. Give each group a story to read and a set of questions to analyze.
- ❏ Have groups trade sets of questions and confirm or challenge the analysis. Circulate within the groups and assist with discussion of challenges.
- ❏ As a large group confirm where there is consensus. Determine correct types if there are questions for which a consensus could not be reached.

Q Tip

Further resources about the ReQuest strategy:
- *Asking Better Questions* by Norah Morgan and Juliana Saxton (1994)
- http://www.education.tas.gov.au/ english/norah.htm#ques

How can I help students create questions for specific purposes?

Q Task
Students will engage in the questioning process using the ReQuest strategy to create questions specific to need.

Clarifying the Task
Students have already been introduced to the ReQuest strategy and have had practice classifying questions using this method. In this task, students will learn to develop their own questions using this process. This is a cross-curricular strategy and can be used with all types of texts; e.g., magazine articles, textbook passages, novels, press releases, etc.

Building Understanding
- Select a short article or story for modeling the task. Prepare the text for projection and provide each student with a copy as well.
- Review the three types of questions: On the Line, Between the Lines, and Beyond the Line.
- Team up students and use the Think, Pair, Share strategy to develop questions. Ask students to individually think of On the Line questions, discuss with their partners, and share one question with the class. Confirm that the question can indeed be answered from the text and chart a few of the questions. There could be endless numbers of On the Line questions, so set a time limit.
- Ask for Between the Lines questions using the same process. Again, when questions are shared, confirm that there is enough information in the text for an inference to be developed. Record several of these questions.
- Finally, ask for Beyond the Line questions. Confirm that the questions shared will extend thinking of the implications about the text. Chart questions.
- Continue modeling with different texts until students are ready to try it on their own.

Demonstrating Understanding
Provide each student with a text and the What's Your Question Line? organizer (page 41). Have students read the text and develop all three types questions.

Q Tip
One benefit of this strategy is the potential to match individual reading abilities with specific texts, enabling all learners to be successful.

What's Your Question Line?

Student name: _____

Title of Text: _____

On the Line __?__	Between the Lines __?__	Beyond the Line → ?

I would like to know more about...

Perhaps I can...

How can coding questions help students look for the answers?

Q Task
Students classify questions by identifying where or how to find the answers.

Clarifying the Task

In this task, students will build on their knowledge of categorizing questions (see ReQuest strategy Q Task, page 39). Classifying questions helps students develop the reading comprehension skills of making connections and inferences. Students first learn to identify questions by determining how they would find the answers, and then learn to apply that knowledge and understanding to create questions. Apply this strategy to articles, textbook excerpts, and video.

Building Understanding

Model the process.

- Source a current article or textbook selection that supports a curriculum topic being studied and create several of each type of question on the Question Codes chart.

Question Codes		
Codes	**Description**	**Solution Strategy**
?	On the Line	Skim text
$\overline{?}$	Between the Lines	Read Text; look for clues; make inferences
→?	Beyond the Line	Study text; make connections
(thought bubble)	Background Knowledge	Think about what you and group members already know; discuss to find answer
☑	Research	Check other sources; make inquiries

Q Tip
Students can apply this strategy when reading both fiction and non-fiction text. Provide students with sticky notes so they can record and code questions as they read.
- This strategy was inspired by ReQuest Procedure (Manzo, 1969) and Categorizing Questions (Harvey and Goudvis, 2000).
- For additional information see *Strategies That Work* by Stephanie Harvey and Anne Goudvis (2000).
- Another approach to explore is Question Answer Relationship (QAR), developed by T.E. Raphael (1984).To learn more see http://www.justreadnow.com/ strategies/qar.htm

- Explain the codes and tell how they assist us to source answers to our reading questions. Share the article and questions with students, and ask them to identify the appropriate code for each question. Ask students to provide an explanation for their classification.

Demonstrating Understanding

Provide students with copies of another curriculum-related text and questions. Have students work first individually to identify the correct codes, then in small groups to compare and discuss their findings. Remind students to refer to the Question Codes chart and questions already classified in the modeling sample as they work. Ask each group to select a "reporter" to provide the group's classification and rationale. Randomly ask groups to share as you discuss each question, asking others to share their rationale if there is dissent.

de Bono's Six Thinking Hats

Edward de Bono's structured thinking strategy Six Thinking Hats (© 1985) is recognized in education as an effective technique to engage students in critical and creative thinking. Introduce students to this technique of thinking and give them lots of practice using it. Apply Six Thinking Hats to developing questions for specific purposes. (http://www.edwdebono.com/)

Six Thinking Hats Summary

White Hat — the neutral hat. White Hat thinking identifies the facts and details of a topic.

Black Hat — the judgmental hat. Black Hat thinking examines the negative aspects of a topic.

Yellow Hat — the optimistic hat. Yellow Hat thinking focuses on the positive and logical aspects of a topic.

Red Hat — the intuitive hat. Red Hat thinking looks at a topic from the point of view of emotions and feelings.

Green Hat — the new ideas hat. Green Hat thinking requires imagination and lateral thinking.

Blue Hat — the metacognition hat. Blue Hat thinking encompasses and reflects on all the other hats looking at the big picture.

Current Events

Post or project a current-event headline and summary for students to read. Instruct students to create six questions about the current event on the Six Thinking Hats organizer (page 44). If you choose to use this strategy as daily bell work, focus on a different hat each day.

Documentary Response

As students view and review a documentary about a curriculum-related issue or event, have them keep track of their questions using the Six Thinking Hats organizer.

Jigsaw

As students prepare to select a focus for research, have them process their ideas by working in Thinking Hat groups, developing questions that meet the criteria for their assigned hat. Jigsaw students in groups of six so each group has a representative of each hat. Instruct students to share questions and select/develop those that would be effective research questions.

Literature Circles

Assign students questioning roles based on the Six Thinking Hats. Each day students take a different Thinking Hat role and develop questions for literature circle discussions.

Match Your Own Color

Have students develop their own color definitions for different types of questions. What is a grey, magenta, or khaki question?

Six Thinking Hats

Create questions about your topic to represent each type of thinking.

White Hat: facts and details

Black Hat: caution and judgment

Yellow Hat: brightness and optimism

Red Hat: emotions and feelings

Green Hat: imagination and creativity

Blue Hat: planning and reflection

Based on de Bono (1985)

What can we learn from famous quotations about questions?

Q Task

Students will study question quotations to learn about the value and purpose of questioning.

Clarifying the Task

It is important for students to understand the value and purpose of asking effective questions. There are many famous quotations about questions and questioning. Becoming familiar with these quotations will help students develop personal understanding of the importance of this skill.

Building Understanding

Develop a collection of good question quotes that are appropriate for your students' comprehension abilities. Select one to model this task.

> Sample of question quote:
>
> *I had six honest serving men*
> *They taught me all I knew:*
> *Their names were Where and What and When*
> *And Why and How and Who.*
> Rudyard Kipling

Ask students what they think this quotation means. Discuss how this quotation might help them become better questioners. Chart their responses.

Demonstrating Understanding

❑ Select and print several quotations on strips of paper.
❑ Have students work with a partner. Each pair has a quotation strip to analyze. Ask students to think about this quotation and discuss what it means. Have them talk about how this quotation might help them become better questioners.
❑ Ask each group to share their understanding of their quotation. Post the quotation strips around the room or on a bulletin board.
❑ Provide each student with the Quotable Question Quotes organizer (page 46). Instruct students to select their favorite quotation from the ones presented and analyze it using the question prompts.

Q Tip

Invite students to bring more question quotations to class as they discover them. Remind students to always credit the author of the quote. Some sources of question quotes to get you started:
Wisdom Quotes: Quotations to Inspire and Challenge
http://www.wisdomquotes.com/cat_questions.html
World of Quotes: Historic Quotes and Proverbs
http://www.worldofquotes.com/topic/Questions/1/
Brainy Quotes
http://www.brainyquote.com/quotes/keywords/questions.html

??? Quotable Question Quotes ???

What is your favorite question quote?

by_____

What do you think it means?

How will it help you to be a better questioner?

Can you make the quote visual? Try a sketch, word web, or cartoon.

3. Learning to Question

Why do we need to be good questioners?

The art of crafting good questions is key to both teaching and learning. Being able to create probing questions empowers both teachers and students. Questioning is a lifelong learning skill that is critical for success in the 21st century.

Who needs to be a good questioner? Teachers, students, researchers, pollsters, interviewers, planners, journalists, diagnosticians, mechanics, technicians, repair people, doctors, nurses, personal trainers, designers, builders, architects, salespeople, travelers, tourists, consumers, investigators, inspectors, parents, lawyers, etc. Asking effective questions is an important life skill.

What is a good question? There are many different types of questions. Basically a good question is the one that gets us the information we need at any given time. Sometimes the answer will be a simple "yes" or "no"; however, on other occasions it will be much more complicated and so will the question that is required to prompt that answer. A good research question is one that guides the questioner through a quest to build personal meaning and understanding. Again this can be very simple or very complex.

Where does questioning belong in the curriculum? The role of questioning runs throughout the curriculum. Motivation to learn is often spurred on by questions. Clarifying details and thoughts, developing understanding, sourcing information, and selecting relevant information are among the many skills crucial to all disciplines that depend on effective questioning skills. Critical thinking, regardless of the subject content, depends on the ability to ask effective questions. The need for questioning skills is ubiquitous.

When do we teach questioning strategies? In the primary years we teach students to differentiate between statements and questions. We also introduce them to the "5 W's." We need continue to take a systematic approach to teaching questioning skills. It is crucial is that questioning skills are introduced and taught formally (Ciardiello, 1998). Regardless of the grade level, take time to observe and assess student skill levels so that you can intervene with appropriate learning experiences.

How do we teach students to become good questioners? What tools can we use to help develop and hone questioning skills? The following tasks are designed to help you do just that.

- How can the "5 W's and How" help students in Question Trekking?
- How can I help students organize data?

- How can questioning help students explore a topic?
- Q Task Quickies: KWL Quickies
- How can creating a question web help students develop a focus?
- How can I introduce the Question Builder to students?
- How can the Question Builder be used to help guide research?
- Q Task Quickies: Using the Question Builder
- How will a rubric help students create better research questions?
- How can students narrow and focus their questions?
- Q Task Quickies: Power-Up Q Cards
- How do I help students create a statement of purpose?
- How do students get to the right question?
- How can I help students move from question to thesis statement?

"The important thing is not to stop questioning." Albert Einstein

---

How can the "5 W's and How" help students in Question Trekking?

Q Task
Students will apply basic question starters to develop questions specific to their need.

Clarifying the Task
In this example, the class is beginning a study of mechanisms and structures. They are to go on a trek in their neighborhood searching for interesting mechanisms and structures. As they observe these sites, they will keep a record of the questions they have about them.

Building Understanding
Model this task by showing students an interesting mechanism, such as specialized kitchen or garden tool, they may not be too familiar with.
- Pass the tool around the classroom for students to examine.
- Review the question starters: *who*, *what*, *when*, *where*, *why*, and *how*.
- Give students time to think about what they know about the topic the tool relates to and what they are curious about.
- Chart what students know and what questions they have. As you chart their questions, highlight the question starters and encourage students to develop their questions using all five starter words.

Demonstrating Understanding
Prepare students for their trek in the neighborhood. Provide each student with copies of the Question Trekking organizer (page 50) so they can keep good records of their discoveries and questions. Students will make a quick sketch, and jot down what they know and questions they have about the mechanism. You will need to plot out the walk ahead of time, making sure that students will be able to spot a variety of mechanisms and or structures on the route you take.

Q Tip
An extension of this task would make an excellent homework assignment: gather background information about other topics such as animal habitats, transportation, uses of electricity, etc.

Question Trekking

Sketch	What I Know

Questions I Have

Who
What
When
Where
Why
How

How can I find answers to my questions?

How can I help students organize data?

Clarifying the Task

In this example, the class is studying nocturnal animal life. They have read stories, viewed videos, and talked about nocturnal animals. Now they are ready to select an animal they are curious about and search for more information. This simple Q Task provides a framework for young and inexperienced researchers to organize their findings.

Building Understanding

- Once students have selected an animal, ask them to fold a paper in half to create a T-chart. Have students brainstorm everything they know about their topic and record the information on the left side of the chart. Then ask students to brainstorm all the questions they have about the nocturnal animal they have selected, and record the information on the right side of the chart. You can prompt their thinking with cards that have question starter words (e.g., *Who, What, Where, When, Why, How*) printed on them.
- Ask students to find a partner, share their questions, and talk about which questions would be good search questions. Have students eliminate or revise any questions that would have one-word answers. Each student should select four good search questions and record them on the My Search Record organizer (page 52).
- Arrange for students to search in the school library for resources that will help them answer their questions. Review strategies for evaluating the usefulness of a resource. Students should select four resources that will help them find answers to their search questions. Encourage students to select a variety of sources if possible; e.g., books, encyclopedias (both print and electronic), web sites, magazine, etc.

Demonstrating Understanding

Assist students with the process of using their questions to guide their searches.

❏ Model for them how to find keywords in their questions that will help them to use tables of contents and indexes to target the information they need.

❏ Review how to skim and scan and how to take jot notes.

❏ Return to the My Search Record organizer and instruct students to use each resource, focusing on only the questions they have recorded as they make their notes in the appropriate boxes.

Q Tip

Students may not find information to answer all their questions in every source; make sure they know that this is okay. They may find conflicting information in the sources they have. This is a great teachable moment to talk about the importance of using more than one resource, and the need to make sure sources are up-to-date and reliable.

My Search Record

Topic: _____

Name: _____

Sources Questions	1		2		3		4	
1)								
2)								
3)								
4)								

How can questioning help students explore a topic?

Q Task

Students will use questions to guide their exploration of a new topic.

Clarifying the Task

In this example, students will be studying the impact of European explorers on North America. Students need to gain some general knowledge of explorers before they embark on their own voyage of discovery. In this Q Task, students will explore a variety of resources to discover general information about a number of European explorers.

Building Understanding

- Introduce the topic of European explorers with a short video clip and establish the time period and some general knowledge about Europe and North America at the time. Ask students what they know already about European explorers. Chart their ideas.
- Introduce the question starters *Who*, *What*, *When*, *Why*, and *Where*. Ask students to think of what they need to know about European explorers. Chart their questions.
- Ask students where they can find information about European explorers and chart their responses. Ask students for keywords that would help them target information they need. Collaboratively develop a list of key words students will use for their searches.

Demonstrating Understanding

❏ Introduce the resource stations (print encyclopedia, electronic encyclopedia, books, pictures, and video) set up in the library. Provide students with blank copies of Quick Fact Trading Cards (page 54).

❏ Instruct students to rotate through the stations. They will skim, scan, read, view, and listen to variety of carefully selected resources and complete as many trading cards as possible in the time available.

❏ Now help students make connections.
- Have students gather in small groups and sort their trading cards alphabetically by explorer's last name.
- Have students sort their cards chronologically, by departure point, by destination, and then by reason for the excursion.
- Have them share the quick facts they recorded on their cards and take note of any conflicting data.
- Ask groups to share how they sorted their cards, to point out interesting connections or patterns they see, as well as conflicting information. Discuss how to verify information when you have a conflict.

Students now have a working background knowledge. They should be ready to decide on a focus for further investigation of European explorers.

Q Tip

Students need to have background knowledge before they can develop questions about a topic. For other ideas on building background knowledge see Koechlin and Zwaan (2005 and 2004), and Marzano *Building Background Knowledge for Academic Achievement* (2005).

Quick Fact Trading Cards

Quick Fact Trading Cards

Who?

What?

When?

Where?

Why?

Quick Fact Trading Cards

Who?

What?

When?

Where?

Why?

Quick Fact Trading Cards

Who?

What?

When?

Where?

Why?

Quick Fact Trading Cards

Who?

What?

When?

Where?

Why?

KWL Quickies

KWL is a tried and true technique for developing students' metacognitive skills. It also confirms for students that learning is a thinking process and that there are steps to take when trying to comprehend something new. Developed by Donna M. Ogle in the 1980s as a strategy to encourage active reading of expository text, this strategy — like all good teaching strategies — has increased in value and diversified in application over time. One of the many benefits of this strategy is that it values student questioning. We have provided a few variations for you to consider.

Exploring a Topic

Successful research is built on the opportunity to explore a topic and to build a knowledge base from which inquiry can sprout. Use KWL after activating prior knowledge with a story, video clip, scavenger hunt, speaker, etc. There are many ways to implement the strategy.
- The KWL Chart (page 58) can be built collaboratively on chart paper.
- In the K column, record information students already know about the topic.
- In the W column, record what students want to know or what they wonder about.
- Provide students with exploratory experiences, such as browsing through books and selected Internet sites.
- In the L column, record new information students have learned.

Students can complete KWL charts individually, but be sure that you build in opportunity for students to talk about what they are recording. Debrief by asking students how the KWL chart has helped them gain interest in the topic.

Preparing for Research

Before students embark on a search to find information for their research project, they need to get their thoughts organized and make some plans. The KNoWLedge organizer (page 60) will spur questioning, and will help students activate prior knowledge, identify sources, and focus on keywords to guide searches. When students complete this organizer, they will be ready to use their searching time more efficiently and will have more time for actually processing the information they find.

Assessment

- Before starting a unit, use the KWL strategy as a diagnostic assessment of student knowledge about a topic.
  - ❏ Have students record what they think is important about the topic in the first column of a KWL Chart (page 58) and questions they have in the second column.
  - ❏ In the third column, have students make a web of their understanding about this topic.
- Post-unit, have students complete another KWL Chart. Have students compare their pre- and post-unit KWLs and write a reflection about their growth.

KWL Quickies (continued)

Comprehending Text

KWL is an engaging alternative to note-taking and is a true demonstration of comprehension of text.

- Select an article or textbook passage to support the curriculum topic.
- Develop an anticipation-guide activity to provide clues to the reading passage and activate thinking about the topic.
- After this introduction, ask students to record what they think is important and relative to this topic in the K column of a KWL Chart (page 58).
- Give them some time to think, and then have them develop questions they would like to find answers to in the W column.
- Remind students to use their question-building skills to develop different kinds of questions, such as fact gathering, analysis, reflective, and predicting questions.
- Ask students to read the text, keeping their assumptions and questions in mind. As they read, instruct them to record what they are learning in the L column.
- After reading, have students meet with a partner, compare their learning, and revisit the text as necessary to confirm information or understanding.
- Debrief with the entire class, discussing their new knowledge as well as how the KWL process helped them comprehend the text.

Science Projects

Use the KWHLQ Chart (page 61) to track growth during a science project. Students use the H column for recording plans for how they will find out what they need to know. The reflective Q box is for new questions.

Problem Solving and Decision Making

Use the KWHLQ Chart (page 61) to provide structure to the difficult processes of problem solving and decision making.

- Try it out collaboratively to explore classroom and playground problems, such as bullying, vandalism, littering, etc.
- Demonstrate how the KWHLQ can be tool to help when making decisions, such as making major purchases.
- Let students apply KWHLQ to solve problems and make personal decisions such as career choices.

KWL Quickies (continued)

Storybook Wishes

- Use the KWW Chart (page 59).
- Show the cover of well-illustrated picture book and ask students to tell you what they know about the story from reading the illustration on the cover.
- Record responses in the K column.
- Now picture walk though the book, asking students to read the pictures and tell you what they know from the illustrations
- Before reading, invite students to ask questions about the story and record these in the middle Wonder column.
- After completing the reading, go back and confirm the ideas recorded in the K column, or correct incorrect assumptions.
- Revisit the middle Wonder questions and see if you discovered the answers to all the student questions in the story.
- Now ask students to think about the events in the story and think about anything they would like to change. Record their thoughts in the Wish column.

Compare Fact and Fiction

Use the KWL Chart (page 58) when comparing fact and fiction.

- After reading fictional stories, say, about monkeys, record the characteristics of monkeys identified in the stories in the K column of a large group chart.
- Discuss how authors of fiction give animals attributes that aren't consistent with real animals. In the W column, list the attributes from fiction that they question.
- Explain the purpose of non-fiction materials and the difference between fact and fiction. Share selected non-fiction books and/or video clips on the topic.
- In the L column, list the factual characteristics of monkeys identified from the resources. Review the K column and confirm and highlight fictional characteristics of monkeys. Students would now be ready to use an organizer to record similarities and differences between monkeys in fiction and monkeys in non-fiction.

KWL Chart

Know	**W**onder	**L**earn

KWW Chart

What I/we **K**now	What I/we **W**onder	What I/we **W**ish

KnoWLedge

What do I **K**now	What do I **n**eed to know	**W**here can I find information

What keywords and phrases will Lead me to information I need?

Adapted from Koechlin and Zwaan, 1997.

KWHLQ Chart

What do I **K**now?	What do I **W**ant to know?	**H**ow will I find out?	What did I **L**earn?

Questions I have now	Next Steps

How can creating a question web help students develop a focus?

Q Task
Students will brainstorm and web questions about a topic.

Clarifying the Task
In this example, students will use the background knowledge on European explorers they build in the Q Task on page 53.

In this Q Task, students work collaboratively to explore the breadth and depth of the topic and use this experience to narrow down the large topic to a focus for their personal inquiry.

Building Understanding
Introduce the Question Storming strategy and model how to use it.

- Brainstorm for questions about a topic students are familiar with; for example, transportation. Use a data projector and commercial software, acetate on an overhead projector, or chart paper to begin building a web of questions about transportation.
- Then brainstorm for more questions about the original questions, and record them with arrows from the original questions. Continue to expand the web as long as questions flow.

You may need to model this strategy with several topics, as students are used to brainstorming for what they know, but are not accustomed to brainstorming for what they need and want to know in the form of questions.

Demonstrating Understanding
- ❏ Ask students to meet in small groups with others who are interested in the same European explorer. Have them develop questions using the Webbing Questions worksheet (page 63).
- ❏ Remind students that they are not brainstorming what they know, but rather what they want to know in the form of questions. Also, the questions need to build out from the original question.
- ❏ In groups, they will share questions with the class. Have students revisit their trading cards from the Q Task on page 54, and consider the group questions to help them settle on the aspects of European exploration or the particular explorer(s) they want to investigate.
- ❏ Have them individually complete a Webbing Questions organizer and select a few questions they are interested in exploring further.

Q Tip
To add a tactile dimension, have students brainstorm questions on sticky notes so they can move their questions around.

Webbing Questions

Write your topic in the centre starburst. Record questions you have about this topic in the surrounding ovals. Continue to develop questions about these questions to further explore and refine your topic.

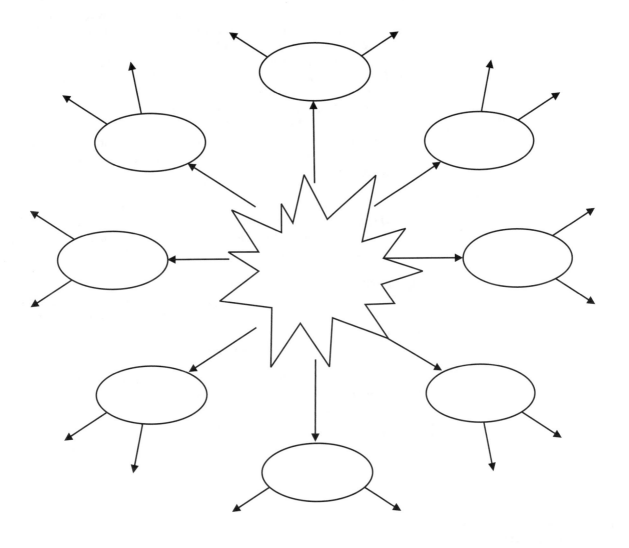

Which questions would you really like to explore for your research project?

Adapted from Koechlin and Zwaan (2005).

How can I introduce the Question Builder to students?

Q Task

Students will learn the structure of the Question Builder Chart (page 65).

Clarifying the Task

This task will help students learn about a structure and pattern of questioning they can use to experiment with in developing their own questions. The purpose of the Question Builder Chart (inspired by the Q Matrix in Weiderhold, 1995) is to give students question starters or prompts to help them construct questions for specific purposes.

Building Understanding

In this example, the class is working on a theme unit on Leaving Home.

- Select a picture book. Show the cover and initiate discussion. Invite students to ask questions. Record the questions.
- Read to a climactic point in the story and ask for more questions. Record.
- Finish the story, review, and discuss recorded questions. Again ask for further questions. Record.
- Review all the generated questions for the purpose of learning more about different kinds of questions and their purposes.
- Clip questions from the chart and ask students to look for similarities.
- Cluster by question starter: *who, what, when, where, why, how,* or *which.*
- Instruct students to look at the second word of each question: *is, are, were, would, will,* etc.
- Use a large wall space to sort and organize questions into a matrix. Discuss which questions were easy to answer and why, which were more difficult, and which had no direct answer in the story but are really interesting questions.

Demonstrating Understanding

- ❏ Group students and provide each group with a large copy of the Question Builder Chart (page 65), or have the students make their own chart on a large piece of chart paper.
- ❏ Instruct students to skim newspapers and magazines to look for questions to clip out.
- ❏ Have students glue the questions they discover onto their chart.
- ❏ Debrief with the entire class and discuss their successes and challenges with this task.

Q Tip

When students are ready, proceed to discuss the purpose of different question starter patterns; see the Q Matrix in Weiderhold (1995). Weiderhold's book and excellent commercial materials to support questioning using the Q Matrix are available from Kagan Cooperative Learning http://www.kaganonline.com/Catalog/index.html
This Q Task was adapted from a task in Koechlin and Zwaan (2004).

Question Builder Chart

	is	did	can	would	will	might
Who						
What						
When						
Where						
How						
Why						
Which...						

Your best questions for this project

Inspired by Weiderhold (1995)

How can the Question Builder be used to help guide research?

Q Task
Students will experiment with the Question Builder Chart (page 65) to formulate focus questions to guide their research tasks.

Clarifying the Task
Students are familiar with the Question Builder Chart. In this example, the class has explored the topic—the world of insects—by taking a nature walk, browsing non-fiction books, viewing videos. They have discussed and recorded interesting discoveries and are now ready to select an insect they are really curious about for their personal search project. This information questioning strategy enables beginning and experienced researchers, as well as students with low language acquisition, to experiment with many possible questions until they find the "just right" question(s) for their project.

Building Understanding
Prepare a large Question Builder Chart (page 65). Model how to use the Question Builder prompts to develop questions.
- Select a topic the class should have some general background knowledge about, such as planning a party or a school event.
- As students volunteer questions, record them directly on the Question Builder. Students will discover that not all the prompts work well for every topic. Caution students not to force questions.
- Ask students to think about which questions might make good research questions. Share and highlight these questions.

Demonstrating Understanding
- ❏ Ensure that each student has selected an insect topic for his or her personal research project. Provide each student with a Question Builder Chart (page 65). Instruct students to experiment with formulating questions about their insects. Have them record their efforts on the chart.
- ❏ Now have students work with a partner to discuss their questions and select the best five for their personal project.
- ❏ Have students construct a search booklet. Have them create a cover and write a guiding question at the top of each page.
- ❏ Students will use teacher-selected resources at their reading level to search for the answers to their questions. They will record the information in their search booklet under the appropriate question.

Q Tip
- Very young students will need a volunteer or a student learning buddy to help them record their discovery questions and read to find answers to their questions. Search findings can be illustrations, or text printed by the learning buddies.
- More experienced researchers can use index cards, folded paper, or templates for organizing their research notes.

Using the Question Builder

Your students will need many opportunities to use the Question Builder prompts. Have them work in small groups at first so they can support each other. When they have had lots of practice experimenting with the prompts they can use the strategy independently to brainstorm questions for specific purposes. The Question Builder Chart (page 65) and Question Builder Frames (page 68) can be adapted for endless applications for all grade levels. The following are examples of using this questioning strategy to critically examine information and develop understanding.

Interpreting Graphs and Charts

As a pre-reading strategy, have students examine charts and/or graphs in a text selection. Using the prompts from the Question Builder Chart or Question Builder Frames, have them develop questions about what they see. Post reading, have students go back to their pre-reading questions and try to answer them. If any of their questions cannot be answered from the text, ask them to develop a plan to try to find the answers.

Analyzing Primary Artifacts

Provide each group of students with a photograph, letter, poster, or other primary artifact that will help them discover firsthand information about the people, places, or events being studied. Ask students to examine and discuss the artifact and, using the prompts from the Question Builder Chart or Question Builder Frames, develop questions about what they see. Have each group share their questions. Chart any common issues or concerns arising from their questions. These ideas could form the focus of further class investigations about the people, places, or events under study.

Looking for Patterns and Trends

Provide students with statistical data; e.g., population breakdowns over a period of time. Have students examine the data and use the Question Builder Chart or Question Builder Frames to develop questions about the data they are examining. Instruct students to swap questions with another group. Answer their questions based on the raw data. Share any patterns they have discovered in the population statistics, as well as potential trends for the future.

Textbook Twist

Note making, answering teacher questions, and completing fill-in-the-blank worksheets from textbook content becomes tedious for students. Occasionally twist the process: instruct students to read the textbook selection and develop some thought-provoking questions about the material they are reading. They can use the Question Builder Chart or Question Builder Frames to experiment with questions, then select their best for sharing as a record of their content understanding.

Question Builder Frames

Who	
is, are, was, were did, does can, could would, should will, might	

What	
is, are, was, were did, does can, could would, should will, might	

When	
is, are, was, were did, does can, could would, should will, might	

Where	
is, are, was, were did, does can, could would, should will, might	

Why	
is, are, was, were did, does can, could would, should will, might	

How	
is, are, was, were did, does can, could would, should will, might	

Which _____	
is, are, was, were did, does can, could would, should will, might	

Inspired by Weiderhold (1995)

How will a rubric help students create better research questions?

Clarifying the Task

In this example, students are preparing to conduct research on issues related to safe drinking water. The teacher will facilitate several exploratory activities. Students will use a rubric to guide them as they create their individual inquiry question(s).

Building Understanding

- Introduce the topic by charting the essential human needs for survival. Discuss what may happen if any or several of these needs are not met.
- Use a video dealing with issues related to safe drinking water to further discussion. Have students use the RVL Connect organizer (page 70) to record their thoughts during the video. Share the student thoughts.
- Collect news articles or passages from texts that deal with water issues, such as unsafe or limited drinking water in various locations in the world, the impact of flooding or other disasters, polluted water, etc. Group students and provide each group with copies of the same article. Ask students to read the article and highlight key passages they are curious about.
- Have students individually record questions they have after reading the article. Have them share with the group, then ask the group to compile a list of questions they feel would make good inquiry questions. Each group then shares the question list. Display question charts.

Demonstrating Understanding

- ❏ Introduce the Your Research Question rubric (page 71). Select a few questions and, with students, rate them using criteria from the rubric. Discuss how to make them better inquiry questions.
- ❏ Have students develop their own individual inquiry questions. Conference with students and use the rubric criteria to make each question as effective as possible.

Q Tip

Your students cannot ask questions when their knowledge of the topic is limited. Educational video is a perfect medium for sparking interest in a topic and providing vital background knowledge. Video can provide vicarious experiences to new worlds for students.

RVL Connect

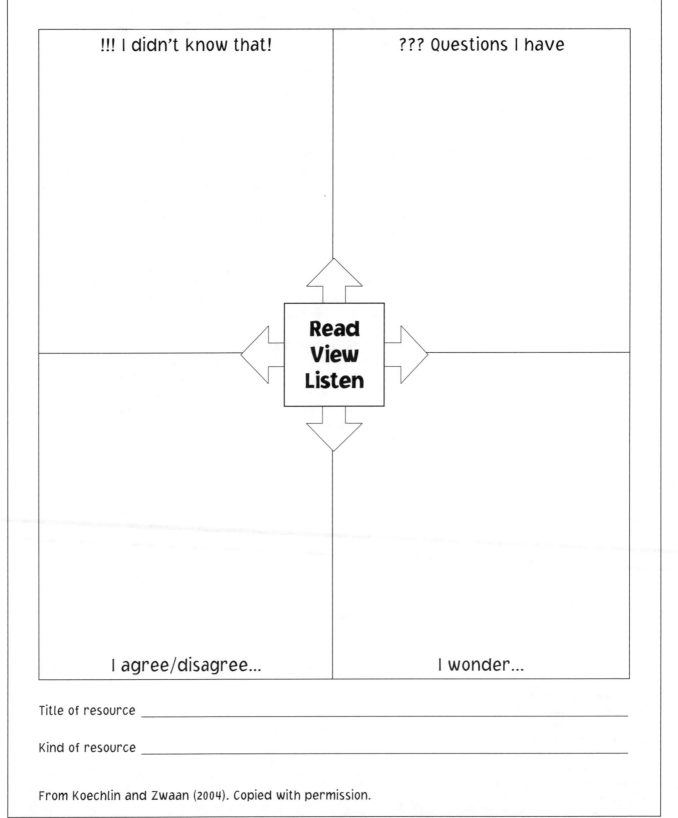

!!! I didn't know that!	??? Questions I have

Read View Listen

I agree/disagree...	I wonder...

Title of resource _____

Kind of resource _____

From Koechlin and Zwaan (2004). Copied with permission.

Your Research Question

Criteria Level	Focus *Does your question help to focus your research?*	Interest *Are you excited about your question?*	Knowledge *Will your question help you learn?*	Processing *Will your question help you understand your topic better?*
Your Research Question:				
Level 4	• focus targets a defined inquiry and examines all relevant perspectives	• inspires further investigation and more questions	• evokes personal action and/or motivates application or transfer	• requires independent analysis, synthesis, and application of information
Level 3	• focus targets a defined inquiry and explores several perspectives	• stimulates curiosity and enthusiasm	• directs personal reflection and opinion	• requires general comparison based on criteria
Level 2	• manageable, with limited exploration potential	• motivates some personal interest	• requires collection of facts and opinions	• requires classification of data
Level 1	• broad and unmanageable or narrow, with little scope	• of little personal interest	• requires lists, one-word answers	• requires data collection only

Comments and Goals

How can students narrow and focus their questions?

Q Task
Students will Power Up inquiry questions for research by using starter and focus words.

❏ Stimulates your curiosity
❏ Guides your research quest
❏ Encourages you to dig deep for information
❏ Challenges you to think about your discoveries
❏ Prompts you to analyze your findings
❏ Helps you make personal meaning
❏ Keeps you focused
❏ Sparks your imagination

Clarifying the Task
In this example, students have been introduced to the topic of natural disasters. They have explored natural disasters through stories, songs, video, books, newspaper articles, pictures, and Internet sites. They are ready to develop their inquiry questions.

Building Understanding
- Review the question starters: *who, what, when, why, where,* and *how.* Review starters for a statement of purpose: *discover, investigate,* and *compare.*
- Introduce the elements of a rich research question (see margin).
- Introduce students to Power-Up words that will help them develop a focused inquiry question. See the Power-up Your Inquiry Question organizer (page 73).
- Highlight question starter words and focus words. Discuss the potential of these questions as rich research questions based on the required elements. Students should be able to see that the focus words help define the inquiry, and that "How" and "Why" question starters always produce rich questions.

Demonstrating Understanding
Using the Power Up Your Inquiry Question organizer (page 73), have each student develop a personal inquiry question(s).

Share sample questions about hurricanes.
- **What** is a hurricane?
- **Investigate** the **kinds** of severe storms and how are they are predicted.
- **Examine** the **consequences** of severe storms for families and businesses.
- **What are** the possible **implications** of recent severe storms for building codes and disaster planning?
- **What** are the **similarities** and **differences** between hurricanes and other types of storms?
- Is there a **connection** between global warming and severity of recent tropical storms?
- **What** can be done to limit the **impact** of severe storms on people, structures and the environment?
- **How** can we ensure that **effective** evacuation and **survival** plans for coping with future disasters are put in place in all vulnerable locations?
- **How might** we **apply** knowledge of design and environmental conditions to improve urban settlement **patterns**?

Q Tip
For further examples of questioning using focus words, see Koechlin and Zwaan (1997).

Power Up Your Inquiry Question

Question starters		Focusing questions			Looking for relationships	
Who	Discover	changes	types	kinds	significance	compare
What	Investigate	jobs	roles	importance	conse-quence(s)	contrast
When	Compare	purpose	structure	characteristics	project	cause
Where	Uncover	value	lifestyle	relationships	implication	effect
Why	Determine	function	defence	adaptations	connection	value
How	Examine	capacity	survival	conditions	correlation	analyze
Which...	Study	intent	result	infer	pattern(s)	
	Research		outcome	imply	trend(s)	

Use this checklist to review your inquiry question(s):	Use one or more of the focus or relationship words in your question to give it research power. Brainstorm your question ideas and record your best efforts here.
❏ Stimulates your curiosity ❏ Encourages you to dig deep for information ❏ Challenges you to think about your discoveries ❏ Prompts you to analyze your findings ❏ Guides your research quest ❏ Keeps you focused ❏ Sparks your imagination ❏ Helps you to make personal meaning	

Review your questions using the checklist above and record your inquiry question(s) here.
Conference with your teacher and teacher-librarian before you begin your quest.

Power-Up Q Cards

Thinking is enhanced and memory reinforced by tactile and visual experiences with information. Turn developing effective research questions into a hands-on as well as minds-on (Wiggins and McTighe, 1998) experience for your students.

Create Packs of Power-Up Q Cards

See the Power Up Your Inquiry Question organizer (page 73). Make a card for each Power-Up word. Handprint them on card stock, or print out several sets at a time using commercial software on business card stock. Print one word on each card. Color code the word if possible; e.g., question starters in green, focus words in blue, relationship words in orange.

Using the Power-Up Q Cards

- Model the process.
- Strategically pre-select a few cards based on the topic being studied.

> If students studying human anatomy, you might give them a pack containing the following assortment.
>
> **Question Starters:** How, What, Discover, Investigate
> **Focus Words:** function, survival, defence, role, purpose, structure
> **Relationship Words:** consequence(s), significance, effect, cause, compare

- Have students work in small groups, using a few of the Power-Up Q Cards to help them create effective research questions. Instruct students to manipulate the cards and experiment with different combinations to spark ideas for good research questions.
- Students should keep a print record of their best questions.

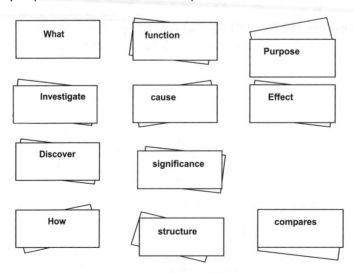

How do I help students create a statement of purpose?

Clarifying the Task

An inquiry does not have to be guided by a formal question with a question mark at the end. A statement of purpose is also a legitimate guide to an inquiry task. In this task, the organizational structure of Bloom's Taxonomy will help students consider the type of thinking that their question or statement of purpose will produce. Although Bloom's Taxonomy is traditionally applied to the questions and tasks teachers ask of students, it is also an understandable structure for discussing levels of thinking with students. Higher-level inquiry is not only possible but desirable in today's information-rich learning environments.

Building Understanding

- Introduce the structure of Bloom's Taxonomy and give students some history of the importance of this work and how much it has influenced education since the mid-1950s.
- Read a popular story, revisit the novel you are reading aloud to your students, or select a thought-provoking article dealing with an issue related to current subject matter.
- Develop a range of sample questions and focus statements you might ask students about the reading material. Ensure that all levels of Boom's Taxonomy are addressed and that students understand what a statement of purpose is (e.g., Discover the role of frogs in a swamp habitat).

Types of Thinking

Knowledge: identification and recall of information
Comprehension: organization, selection, and understanding of facts and ideas
Application: use of facts, rules, and principles in new situations
Analysis: taking information apart and looking for relationships
Synthesis: bringing ideas together to create new patterns and build personal meaning
Evaluation: making judgments and decisions

- Discuss the type of thinking each question or focus statement will generate. Invite students to make up more questions or focus statements.

Demonstrating Understanding

- ❏ Provide students with Categorizing Questions and Focus Statements with Bloom (page 76). Review the categories, prompts, and sample question starters.
- ❏ Group students and give each group a picture book or an article at their interest and developmental level. Instruct students to read and discuss the book and then create a question or task statement for each of Bloom's levels, using the Building Questions and Focus Statements with Bloom organizer (page 77).
- ❏ Have groups exchange books and questions and assess if the questions and task statements match the assigned Bloom category. Discuss discrepancies and any other problems the students encountered.

Categorizing Questions and Focus Statements with Bloom

Knowledge: identification and recall of information

Prompts	Samples
List, Tell, Describe, State, Identify, Label, Recognize	Who/what/when/where...? Describe how... Identify those who...

Comprehension: organization, selection, and understanding of facts and ideas

Prompts	Samples
Relate, Interpret, Summarize, Outline, Infer, Explain, Interpret	What is the main idea...? Explain what is meant by... What are facts? What are opinions?

Application: use of facts, rules, and principles in new situations

Prompts	Samples
Apply, Prepare, Construct, Simulate, Discover, Solve	How is _____ related to_____? Why is _____ significant? Predict what would happen if...

Analysis: taking information apart and looking for relationships

Prompts	Samples
Compare, Sequence, Contrast, Classify, Distinguish, Relate	How does _____ compare/contrast with_____? What's the relationship between _____ and _____? What are the causes and effects of...?

Synthesis: bringing ideas together to create new patterns and build personal meanings

Prompts	Samples
Solve, Develop, Reconstruct, Create, Combine, Design, Rearrange	What might happen if you combined _____ with _____? What solutions can you suggest for...? Develop a plan for... Develop a point of view on ... How does _____ influence _____? What are the alternatives to...?

Evaluation: making judgments and decisions

Prompts	Samples
Recommend, Rank, Prioritize, Appraise, Justify, Defend, Criticize	What is the most important.... and why? Which is better, logical, valid, appropriate? Judge the effects of... Appraise the situation and defend your opinion on...

Based on Bloom (1956)

Building Questions and Focus Statements with Bloom

Knowledge: identification and recall of information	
Prompts	Your Turn
List, Tell, Describe, State, Identify, Label, Recognize	

Comprehension: organization, selection, and understanding of facts and ideas	
Prompts	Your Turn
Relate, Interpret, Summarize, Outline, Infer, Explain, Interpret	

Application: use of facts, rules, and principles in new situations	
Prompts	Your Turn
Apply, Prepare, Construct, Simulate, Discover, Solve	

Analysis: taking information apart and looking for relationships	
Prompts	Your Turn
Compare, Sequence, Contrast, Classify, Distinguish, Relate	

Synthesis: bringing ideas together to create new patterns and build personal meanings	
Prompts	Your Turn
Solve, Develop, Reconstruct, Create, Combine, Design, Rearrange	

Evaluation: making judgments and decisions	
Prompts	Your Turn
Recommend, Rank, Prioritize, Appraise, Justify, Defend, Criticize	

Based on Bloom (1956)

How do students get to the right question?

≣ **Q Task**
Students will develop effective inquiry questions.

Clarifying the Task

Effective inquiry questions or statements of purpose empower students to conduct research that is exciting and meaningful. The purpose is to end the tendency to collect and regurgitate data, and begin the move towards research projects that build understanding, that have personal relevance for the learners and significance for their audience. End plagiarism in your school by teaching students to develop good inquiry questions.

Building Understanding

Model for students how you would use inquiry questions to help you with a task, such as writing an article for a professional journal, planning a special party, or purchasing a new car.

> What are you really curious about?
> Why do you want to explore this topic?
> What do you know already?
> What do you need/want to find out?
> How will you make sense of the data you discover?
> Who will your audience be?
> What do you want your audience to understand about your research?
> How will you share your new learning?

Demonstrating Understanding

❏ Students need lots of practice as well as strategies and tools to help them develop effective research questions. Provide students with many opportunities to experiment with different strategies and tools for constructing questions.

❏ See the organizers provided: Question Stretchers (page 79), Building a Research Focus (page 80), and Focusing My Inquiry (page 81).

❏ When students have narrowed their focus and have some questions to consider, introduce the Inquiry Question Contract (pages 82–83). Have students complete the contract to refine their inquiry question or statement of purpose.

❏ Conference with students and confirm that they are ready to start their research. As students proceed with their research, they may discover that they need to adjust their focus and or their question.

Q Tip
For further exploration regarding building inquiry questions, see Booth (2003) and visit *Questioning.org*, Jamie McKenzie's online journal devoted to questioning at http://questioning.org/

Question Stretchers

Surface questions

	is	did
Who		
What		
When		
Where		

Digging questions

	can	would
Who		
What		
When		
Where		

Digging deeper questions

	will	might
Who		
What		
When		
Where		

Developing understanding questions

	is	did	can	would	will	might
How						
Why						

Building a Research Focus

What do I know already about this topic?

What do I need to consider for this project?

What is my focus now?

What am I curious about?

How do I start my research?

Focusing My Inquiry

What is my general topic? What am I specifically interested in? What am I curious about? What do I already know? What do I need to know?

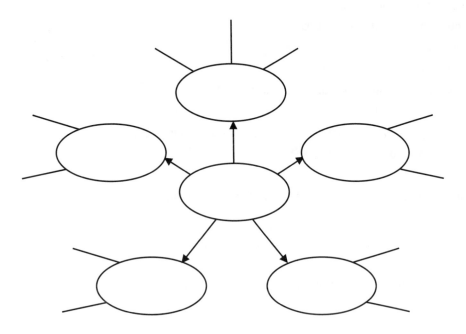

Focus Words: What focus words will enrich my research question?
Which focus words will help me analyze my data?

_____

Inquiry question/statement of purpose:

_____
_____

Subtopics: Which subtopics will help me organize my data?
I predict I will need to explore these categories:

- _____
- _____
- _____
- _____

Changes, types, kinds, jobs, roles, importance, characteristics, structure, purpose, value, function, relationships, lifestyle, adaptations, conditions, defense, survival, compare, contrast, cause, effect, value, significance, consequences, impact, infer, imply, project, analyze, etc.

Keywords

Inquiry Question Contract

Consider these guiding questions as you build your inquiry question:

- What are you really curious about?
- Why do you want to explore this topic?
- What do you know already?
- What do you need/want to find out?
- How will you make sense of the data you discover?
- Who will your audience be?
- What do you want your audience to understand about your research?
- How will you share your new learning?

Complete these statements when you are ready to refine your inquiry focus.

My/our broad topic is _____

I/we am/are specifically interested in _____

_____

_____

because I/we want to find out

_____

_____

_____

I/we want others to (know, understand, learn, try, create, make, etc.)

_____

_____

_____

I/we will share what I/we have learned by

_____

_____

_____

Inquiry Question Contract (continued)

My/our inquiry question or statement of purpose:

_____

_____

_____

I/we understand that this project will be assessed by

_____

_____

_____

To be successful I/we need to:

❏

❏

❏

❏

❏

Student signature _____ Date _____

Teacher signature _____ Date _____

How can I help students move from question to thesis statement?

Q Task
Students will use their guiding research questions and teacher prompts to build a thesis.

Clarifying the Task
A thesis demonstrates a very high level of understanding about a topic. As young researchers mature, they become more adept at this formal synthesis. When students are developmentally ready, usually at the secondary level, teachers require students to prepare academic papers framed by a personal thesis statement. However, the development of a thesis statement should also be a step in the process of preparing any presentation that requires students to synthesize their findings, and present and defend their personal understandings. In this Q Task, students are already well into the research process. They have explored their topic, developed an inquiry question to guide their research, identified appropriate resources, and started gathering and organizing their data. At this point, before students are finished research, the skill of building a thesis should be introduced.

Building Understanding
Project a sample essay on a screen and deconstruct the essay using a think-aloud. Highlight the thesis statement and explain that this statement is usually found at the end of the first paragraph statement.

- Examine the essay for the supporting evidence the author uses to defend the thesis. Point out transition words used to link ideas. Identify the kinds of evidence cited; e.g., cause and effect, similarities and differences, illustrations, relationships, etc. Discuss how effectively the author has delivered the argument, and make suggestions for strengthening the essay.
- Group students and provide each group with a sample essay to deconstruct. Circulate and provide support as students work. Ask each group to share the thesis statement of the essay they were assigned, and to explain how well the author defended their thesis.
- Discuss the elements of an effective thesis and chart student responses: e.g., focused and concise, arguable, supported by effective evidence, original thought, etc. Explain to students that their thesis should pass the "So what?" test; i.e., the thesis should be a strong hook to capture their audience's attention and pique their interest.

Demonstrating Understanding
- ❏ Provide students with the Building Your Thesis Map organizer (page 85). Explain that they will use this organizer to help them move from their research question to a thesis statement. Instruct students to record new questions they have about their topic, as well as the connections they are making as they proceed.
- ❏ Review the question prompts and remind students that visual organizers—concept maps, flow charts, Venn diagrams, etc.—are perfect tools for helping them analyze their data and finding relationships.
- ❏ Conference with students after they develop their possible thesis statement.
- ❏ Conference again when they refine it and prepare to write their essays or develop their multimedia presentation.

Q Tip
Check out these web sites for examples of thesis statements and support to help students as they become more independent in writing a thesis:

The Writing Lab and Owl at Purdue University
http://owl.english.purdue.edu/owl/resource/545/01

What is a Thesis
http://mciu.org/~spjvweb/thesis.html

Building Your Thesis Map

During the research process, you will be working towards your thesis. Your research question will guide you along your journey. As you gather more information, you will probably discover that you have more questions. This organizer provides a process path and prompts to record your valuable thoughts and questions as you build your thesis.

Inquiry question	
New questions	**Reflections and connections**
Question prompts	
Have you explored all relevant perspectives?	What conclusions are you reaching?
Have you discovered any conflicting information?	Have you formed an opinion?
Can you see relationships and patterns building?	What evidence do you have to support your opinion?
What similarities and differences have you found?	Do you need more evidence to defend your position?
What surprises or disturbs you?	Why is your research important?
	Who should know about it/Why?

Possible thesis

I believe/propose/conclude/argue...

Thesis Check Point	**Test out your thesis ideas.**
❏ arguable and supported by evidence	Talk to
❏ probable or defendable	❏ fellow students
❏ specific and effective	❏ teachers
❏ your synthesis	❏ teacher-librarian
❏ original thought	❏ parents
❏ provocative or unique	❏ experts

Continue research and keep refining your thesis.

4. Questioning to Learn

How do good questions empower learners?

Questions can be an effective tool for students. Teacher-created questions, used as a scaffold, empower students to work though a rich learning experience on their own. When students themselves become skilled questioners, able to develop situation-specific questions independently, the positive impact on learning is evident in their achievements. They will develop better understanding, interpret media, probe issues with perception, form personal opinions, see relationships, make connections, draw conclusions; they will be able and adept at higher-level thinking.

The impact of technology has caused educators to take another look at the meaning of literacy and to expand the definition to include information literacies, visual literacy, and digital literacy. For students to be successful in the cyber-world, they need to hone their critical and creative thinking skills. Effective questioning skills are a catalyst for this achievement.

Students who question to learn will take possession of their own intellectual growth. They will apply questioning skills to sort through the information glut, to analyze data, to connect to literature and the arts, to solve problems, to make decisions, to take action, to self-analyze, and to set goals. The question will become their most useful information tool.

Most students need to be taught questioning skills and require lots of practice applying them before they develop independence. In this chapter we have included tasks to provide some of the many possible applications for the tools presented in chapter 3: Learning to Question.

- How can teacher-guided questioning improve experimentation in art?
- Q Task Quickies: The Emotional Line
- How can questions enable students to read visual images?
- How can questioning enable critical analysis of visual text?
- How can I help students identify perspectives and understand opinions?
- How can questioning help form personal opinions?
- How do questions facilitate working with web text?
- Q Task Quickies: Questioning on the Web
- What is the role of questioning in clarifying understanding?
- What is the role of questioning in testing ideas and theories?
- How does a journalist develop interview questions?
- How do students create effective interview questions?
- How can students prepare to effectively question an expert?
- How can primary students create survey questions?
- How can questions enable comparison?
- How do students know which attributes to compare?

- What role do questions play in building understanding?
- How can students use FAQs to demonstrate or share their learning?
- How can peer questioning enhance student creative writing?
- How can we use Book Talking Strategy?

Once you have learned how to ask relevant and appropriate questions, you have learned how to learn and no one can keep you from learning whatever you want or need to know. (Postman and Weingartner, *Teaching as a Subversive Activity*)

How can teacher-guided questioning improve experimentation in art?

Q Task

Students will discover how teacher-guided questioning can help them experiment purposefully to develop line designs with scissors.

Clarifying the Task

In this example, students are engaged in the study of line in art, and will be asked to apply that knowledge while learning to use scissors effectively as an artistic tool. They will consider the characteristics and variety of lines.

Building Understanding

- Ask students to brainstorm what they know about line, and to identify the varieties of lines they could create. Make a list of different kinds of lines: straight, curved, zigzag, diagonal, arcs, spirals, thick, thin, etc.; angles, combinations, etc. Illustrate on the chalkboard.
- Ask questions relating the types of lines to how to create them with scissors:

> - How can you reproduce these line designs using your scissors?
> - What is the best way to cut a smooth curving line?
> - What is the best way to create a zigzag line?
> - When is it better to move the scissors?
> - When is it better to move the paper?
> - How many combinations can you create?

- Allow students time to experiment with newsprint and cut many different examples.
- Add to the list of lines as students discover more line types and combinations.
- Discuss how the guided questioning helps students make discoveries about using scissors to create line design.

Demonstrating Understanding

Review how line can be used to convey a mood in art. Issue a challenge:
- ❏ Can you cut all the line examples and keep the paper sample all in one piece?
- ❏ Create an abstract 3D work of art using the sample piece, with a new piece of paper as background. What do these line forms remind you of? What will you call your creation?

Q Tip

This approach can be applied to other art skills:
- How many ways can you use a crayon?
- How can you create texture when using modeling clay?

Check out some web sites.
http://www.sanford-artedventures.com/study/g_line.html
http://icom.museum/vlmp/galleries.html

The Emotional Line

Part of a student's experimentation with art is understanding the emotional component of even the most simple elements. Using teacher-guided questions, you can help students connect line design to emotions.

Show students slides of artworks using line. Brainstorm for emotions evoked. Use guiding questions to help students connect line and emotion.

- What do you think of when you see this curved spiral? Why?
- How do you feel when you see this thick straight line (fine straight line, thick curving line, fine curving line, thick zigzag line, fine zigzag line, etc.)?
- What do you think of when you see this combination of zigzag and curved lines?
- What does the artist want us to feel when we see these lines converging?
- How has this artist created a sense of power with line?

Discuss how the guiding questions helped them connect line types to feelings.

Reading Between the Lines

Group students and provide them with art prints that demonstrate a variety of line types. Ask students to find different kinds of lines and discuss the emotions evoked by them; for example "smooth, flowing, horizontal lines create a feeling of peace and harmony," "sharp, jagged, vertical lines create a feeling of energy and unease" (Ontario Curriculum, Visual Arts).

Collage of Feelings

- Provide students with colored construction paper, scissors, and glue. Instruct students to apply their knowledge of line to create their own collage of feelings. Allow time for students to present their compositions in small groups.
- Instruct students to apply their questioning skills to discover how each presenter connected emotions and line design.

How can questions enable students to read visual images?

≡ *Q Task*
Students will use and develop questions to help them read illustrations and photographs.

Clarifying the Task

In this example, students will think about what life was like for children in the past. In the 19th century, only the children of the wealthy were educated. Most other children—even the very young—worked at home, in the fields, in mines, and even in factories. Collect archival photographs of children at work in various jobs in the late 19th and early 20th centuries. You could print, reference, and mount them as if in an old album, or select from archival Internet sites and bookmark them.

Building Understanding

- Explore a video about working children to introduce the topic; e.g., *Pit Pony* (Cochran Entertainment) or *Chandler's Mill* (National Film Board of Canada).
- Introduce the guiding question—*What was life like for working children in the late 19th and early 20th centuries?*—and display the photo collection. Display the Picture Prompts to guide their picture reading.

Picture Prompts

- Where is this scene located?
- What is happening now?
- What might have happened just prior to this picture?
- What might happen next?
- Who do you see in the picture?
- Who do you not see that might be involved? Why?
- What does this picture remind you of?

- Allow students time to view all the photos and then select a photo they are curious about. Invite students to step into the picture, to project themselves back in time until they are right there with the child. Ask students to step about inside the photo. What do they see, hear, and smell?
- Have students use the Step In/Step About/Step Out worksheet (page 91) to record their findings and develop lots of questions they want to ask the child in the photo.
- Have students research in the school library to discover as much as possible about the time period, and the work and life of children.

Demonstrating Understanding

❑ Ask students to step out of the photo and use their research notes and the photo to reconstruct a day, or a series of days, in the child's life, using the form of diary entries.
❑ Students can create a museum-type exhibit with the photo, diary entries, and perhaps an artifact, such as a piece of clothing, buttons, a ribbon, or a coin.

Q Tip
See *What do I do about the kid who...? 50 ways to turn teaching into learning* by Kathleen Gould Lundy. (2004)
This Q Task is adapted from Koechlin and Zwaan (2005).

Step In/Step About/Step Out

Step in to the photograph/picture you have selected. Step about and observe your surroundings.

What do you see?	What do you hear?	What do you smell?

Make lists of all the questions you have about the place you are in.

Step out of the photograph or picture now. How can you find the answers to all your questions? Who can help? Make a plan.

From Loertscher, Koechlin, and Zwaan (2005). Copied with permission.

How can questioning enable critical analysis of visual text?

Clarifying the Task
In this example, the class has been studying controversial issues, focusing on sifting fact from innuendo, propaganda, personal opinion, and misinformation. At this point they have a good background on the issue and will begin to consider cartoonists' takes on it.

Building Understanding
- Collect a variety of editorial cartoons dealing with different aspects and perspectives of an issue the students are familiar with.
- Select and project one of these for the class to view. Watch and listen for different reactions from students. Acknowledge that there are valid and different perspectives within the class and that they will result in different reactions. Encourage students to respect and honor their differences.
- Ask students whose reactions were noticeable to share their thoughts and explain what prompted them. Make a chart and record the reaction and what prompted the reaction. Then ask other students to share their responses and continue to build the chart.
- Using the charted information, collaboratively create a list of questions to guide students as they analyze editorial cartoons.

Analyzing Editorial Cartoons

- Whose point of view is represented?
- Who or what will this cartoon influence?
- Whose perspective is missing?
- How did these factors affect your reaction?
- What might you infer from this work?
- How do you feel about it? Why?
- Do others feel differently? Why?
- How does the cartoonist make use of exaggeration?
- How does the cartoonist appeal to emotions?
- What special techniques does the cartoonist use?

Demonstrating Understanding
Mount the cartoons and the analysis questions on chart paper and display on the walls around the classroom. Have students visit each cartoon and use a marker to record their personal responses, graffiti style, on the chart surrounding the cartoon. Remind students to take some think time before reacting. Students continue their "gallery walk" to visit as many cartoon exhibits as time allows.

Q Tip
- Try this before beginning the study of an issue and again at the end of the study. Compare the reactions.
- Visit www.mediaawareness.com for other strategies to critically analyze media texts.

How can I help students identify perspectives and understand opinions?

Q Task

Students will learn how questions help them to identify and understand the opinions of others.

Clarifying the Task

Students are often required to express an opinion on a curriculum-related issue. Everyone has an opinion, but are the opinions expressed really valid? Are they based on fact? Students need to understand to what extent opinions are guided by the amount and quality of information available to them, and by the degree of their understanding. In this task, students will be guided by focus questions to express their opinions about a topic prior to and after viewing a video, and then to assess the impact additional and/or new information had on their opinion.

Building Understanding

- Define opinion. Present the topic: *The US government plans to drill for oil in Alaska.*
- Provide each student with a copy of the Alaskan Oil Opinion Quiz: Pre-viewing (page 94) to fill out prior to viewing the video *Baked Alaska* (Bullfrog Films). Allow time to complete the quiz based on their current knowledge of the issue.
- Distribute and explain how to use the Who Says What? facts and perspectives organizer (page 96). Show the video again and allow time afterwards for students to record their discoveries. Note that an additional viewing or a stop–start viewing may be necessary for some or all students. Facilitate a class discussion of findings.

Demonstrating Understanding

Now that students have this new information, have them complete the Alaskan Oil Opinion Quiz: Post-viewing (page 95). Ask them to compare their pre- and post-viewing responses, and identify where and how their answers changed. Have the class share and chart the changes, and then discuss what it was that caused their opinions to change.

Q Tip

- Start a class collection of issue-based articles from a wide variety of perspectives. Identify the key ideas, the perspective, and factors that influence each. Use these articles for students to practise questioning skills.
- *Baked Alaska*, an award-winning film, produced by Bullfrog films is available on VHS and DVD.

Alaskan Oil Opinion Quiz

Pre-viewing

1. Do North Americans have a need for more oil?   **Yes**   **No**
Why?

2. Is getting oil from Alaskan sources a good idea?   **Yes**   **No**
Why?

3. Would drilling in Alaska cause any serious problems?   **Yes**   **No**
What?

4. Would Americans benefit from Alaskan oil?   **Yes**   **No**
Who?

5. Would Canadians benefit from Alaskan oil?   **Yes**   **No**
Who?

6. Do I support drilling for oil in Alaska?   **Yes**   **No**
Why?

Alaskan Oil Opinion Quiz

Post-viewing

1. Do North Americans have a need for more oil?   **Yes**   **No**
Why?

2. Is getting oil from Alaskan sources a good idea?   **Yes**   **No**
Why?

3. Would drilling in Alaska cause any serious problems?   **Yes**   **No**
What?

4. Would Americans benefit from Alaskan oil?   **Yes**   **No**
Who?

5. Would Canadians benefit from Alaskan oil?   **Yes**   **No**
Who?

6. Do I support drilling for oil in Alaska?   **Yes**   **No**
Why?

Who Says What?

What are the facts to consider?	What are the perspectives?
–	**Stakeholder**
	Perspective
–	Rationale
–	**Stakeholder**
	Perspective
–	Rationale
–	**Stakeholder**
	Perspective
–	Rationale
–	**Stakeholder**
	Perspective
–	Rationale
–	So what? What do I think about it now?
–	

How can questioning help form personal opinions?

Clarifying the Task
Forming an opinion is an information process. Students will learn that developing an informed opinion is based on identifying and researching all relevant perspectives on an issue, followed by critical thought and consideration.

Building Understanding
Students have completed an in-depth study of an issue. They are preparing to write a position paper.
- To help students form a personal opinion about this issue, provide them with guiding question prompts such as:

- What is the problem or issue in debate?
- What are the important perspectives to consider?
- What arguments are presented by the stakeholders?
- What contradictions or inconsistencies did you uncover, if any?
- What are the actual facts regarding these inconsistencies?
- How do you react to these facts? Why do you feel this way?

- After students have considered their answers to the questions, distribute the Take a Position Line worksheet (page 98). Instruct them to think about where they see themselves on the position line.
- Have students identify four important stakeholders in the issue being considered— candidates, journalists, lobbyists, government, environmentalists, home owners, students, etc.—and mark where each would sit on the line. Then have students identify and mark their personal location on the line.

Demonstrating Understanding
Instruct students to draft their position paper using the guiding questions and their position line as a framework for their writing. Have students work with a partner and exchange papers to edit each other's draft work. Again, instruct students to refer to the guiding questions as they peer edit.

Q Tip
For ideas on using the Take a Position Model see Koechlin and Zwaan (2004).
Give students lots of practice with this process of forming an opinion so that the process will become intuitive.

Take a Position Line

↑

Against
negative
no
Unique Position

For
Affirmative
Yes
Prevalent Position

My position is _____

because _____

How do questions facilitate working with web text?

Q Task

Students will develop questions and apply tips for reading and working with web text.

Clarifying the Task

In this sample, the class is preparing to conduct independent study of issues related to air quality. This task will give students opportunities to explore many aspects of air quality, such as smog, car emissions, ozone, heath concerns, etc. Students will explore selected web sites with teacher-developed guiding questions, and keep track of their learning and new questions as they travel from site to site.

Building Understanding

- Collect news clips and/or articles related to air-quality issues. View/read these current news items and dialogue with students to begin building background information.
- Inform students that you want them to gain further insight into multiple issues by exploring some selected web sites. Ask students to explain how they find information they need on sites that are new to them.
- Record their ideas and introduce the Tips for Reading Web Text list (page 100). Model the tips suggested by exploring a web site and voicing your thoughts and questions as you explore.

Demonstrating Understanding

- ❏ Provide copies of the Air Quality E-tour (page 101) and prepare students for the tour. Remind them to review their Tips for Reading Web Text and to follow the E-tour itinerary.
- ❏ Students will record their findings on the Air Quality E-tour Map worksheet (page 102) and keep track of their own personal questions as they tour the web sites. This tour will give students a working knowledge of important issues so they will be able to select an aspect they are personally interested in exploring for independent study.

Q Tip

It is very easy to get lost in the sea of information available on many web sites. The best way to stay on course is to develop questions that serve as guideposts. These questions can be teacher-developed at first. Students need to keep revisiting these questions as they work their way through the site, to make sure they do not wander off track and waste valuable time.

This Q Task is adapted from Loertscher, Koechlin and Zwaan (2005).

Tips for Reading Web Text

- What is your purpose? Why are you reading?
  - ❏ To find specific facts (dates, weather, statistics)
  - ❏ To conduct research about a topic
  - ❏ To prepare for a class discussion
  - ❏ For fun and relaxation

- Preview the page to gain an overview.
- Pick up bits of data that catch your eye.
- Skim read the titles and subtitles.
- Use the scroll bar to see the entire page.
- Check out the tabs and any other contents lists or tools.
- Connect with what you already know.
- Predict what you think you will learn.
- Decide if this is a good source for you.

- **Jot down some questions about things you hope to discover.**
- Use these questions to focus your navigation so you won't waste time. **Your guiding questions will keep you on track.**
- Make use of visual information (pictures, maps, charts, graphs, etc.)
- Look for sidebars and captions (summary points, important facts, see also references, etc.)
- Look for bolded words, colored text to indicate key information and hyperlinks.
- Navigate the text and the site using tools available.
- **Review your guiding questions frequently.**
- Read for needed detail.
- Return to the home page if the data is off topic and try another link.
- Keep point notes and sketches as you navigate and read.
- Record site URL or bookmark it so you can return easily.

Have you answered all your questions?

Do you need to find another site to confirm your findings?

Do you have more questions?

Air Quality E-tour

Exploring Smog

Selected Web Sites

Environment Canada: Let's talk about health and air quality
http://www.hc-sc.gc.ca/hecs-sesc/air_quality/talk.htm#3
Environment Canada: Clean Air On Line
http://www.ec.gc.ca/cleanair-airpur/Home-WS8C3F7D55
-1_En.htm
Air Now: Air Quality Index (AQI)
http://www.epa.gov/airnow/aqi.html
*Earth Observatory: Study reveals smog clearing properties
of atmosphere*
http://earthobservatory.nasa.gov/Newsroom/MediaAlerts/
2005/2005051218981.html
Pollution Probe: Air Quality
http://www.pollutionprobe.org/Publications/Air.htm
US Air Quality
http://alg.umbc.edu/usaq/
Canadian Health Portal: Environmental Health
http://chp-pcs.gc.ca/CHP/index_e.jsp/pageid/4005/odp/Top/
Health/Environmental_Health/Air_Quality/Smog

Tour Check

- Review guiding questions.
- Stick to the tour itinerary.
- Check off sites visited.
- Skim and scan for needed data.
- Keep notes as you go.
- Record direct quotes you find useful with proper citations.
- Make use of hypertext links within the web site for further detail.
- Use the Back button to return to original site, or look for a link to the Home Page if you get lost.
- Revisit the guiding questions and continue touring until you have fulfilled your exploration.

Guiding Questions

What is smog?
What are the components of smog?
What causes smog to develop?
Where does smog occur most often?
When is smog most likely to occur?
What are the biggest contributors to the occurrence of smog?
How is smog detected and measured?
How does smog affect people? the environment?
How do the effects of smog influence on the health care system, the economy,
the workforce, the environment?
What effect do weather systems have on where smog is created
and where it appears?

Air Quality E-tour Map

When is smog most likely to occur?

Where does smog occur most often?

What are the biggest contributors to the occurrences of smog

How does smog affect
–people?

What is smog?

How do the effects of smog affect
–the health care system?

–the economy?

–the workforce?

–the environment?

–the environment?

How is smog detected and measured?

What are the major components of smog?

What effect do weather systems have on where smog is created and where it appears?

Questioning on the Web

E-Tours

Your students can create their own e-tours (see pages 99–102) as a presentation/product to demonstrate their understanding of a topic, and their ability to navigate the Internet and select the best web resources to support their topic. Students will develop guiding questions to help their readers uncover important information and develop their own understanding of the topic or issue.

Scavenger/Treasure Hunts

This web activity—essentially a fact-finding mission—is usually used when teachers want to give novice web users practice in navigating the web and using search tools effectively. Turn the tables by inviting students to demonstrate their new web navigational skills in the creation of their own scavenger hunts and treasure hunts for other students to complete. The strategy can also be used to build background information about a topic: instruct students to explore web sites and evaluate them to select the best, and then develop factual questions for students to discover the answers to. For more information, see *Scavenger Hunts: Searching for Treasure on the Internet* http://www.education-world.com/a_curr/curr113.shtml

WebQuests

A well-crafted WebQuest is an engaging inquiry experience that allows students to use the potential of the web to make quick links to the best information. An effective WebQuest poses a problem or question for students to explore and provides adequate learning advice to prompt analysis and synthesis. The conclusion should raise more questions and spark further investigation. There are many teacher-developed WebQuests on the web; many are able to elevate students to think critically and creatively.

For more information, see the following:
- *The WebQuest Page - Bernie Dodge* http://webquest.sdsu.edu/
- *Best WebQuests* http://bestwebquests.com/

Comparisons

This activity is useful for helping students understand that some sources of information are better than others, depending on the specific needs they have. Instruct students to create their own questions for comparing two resources. Encourage students to experiment making lots of questions using tools such as the Question Builder Frames on page 68. Students could compare
- web sites on the same topic
- a web site and a book
- online encyclopedias
- an online encyclopedia and a print encyclopedia
- search engines

What is the role of questioning in clarifying understanding?

Clarifying the Task

In this example, students have completed individual research about an environmental problem or issue. Each has developed a personal inquiry question, conducted research, analyzed findings, and prepared a two-minute report to share his or her discoveries. Students will present their research findings in an expert-panel format. Each panel will consist of four or five students.

Building Understanding

- Before the experts present their reports, inform the class that everyone will be expected to contribute to developing deeper understanding of the issues presented. Each student will apply active listening skills and prepare to ask questions of each expert.
- Introduce the I Need to Know More organizer (page 105) and explain the process by modeling it yourself.
  - Prepare a two-minute report on a topic of interest to you and present it to your class.
  - Ask students to jot down key words or sketches as they listen, and then prepare a few questions they would like to ask to clarify their understanding.
  - For the purpose of this demonstration, allow time for a number of questions.
  - Discuss and chart tips for the questioners, and develop a list of response prompts to help the experts respond to questions.

Response prompts for expert panelists

- Let me rephrase your question…
- If I understand your question correctly…
- It is an interesting question; however, I did not…
- I cannot answer that; however, I can recommend a book, web site, etc.
- I am sorry, I did not encounter this issue in my research; however,…
- In my opinion…
- Based on my research…
- According to the sources I checked…
- I like your question and I will try…

Demonstrating Understanding

Review the logistics for the expert-panel session.

- ❏ Each expert has two minutes; they can each take only three questions from the audience.
- ❏ Everyone in the audience keeps a log of their responses and questions as they listen to each expert. See the I Need to Know More organizer (page 105).
- ❏ The questioner needs to address the expert the question is for: "This question is for _____."
- ❏ A moderator will ensure that everyone has a chance to ask at least one question.

Q Tip

- Make the experience as authentic as possible: set up a central podium and microphone for questions; or arrange to telephone, e-mail, or text message questions to the experts.
- See the Questioning Etiquette and Guidelines chart on page 110.

I Need to Know More

Speaker _____   Topic _____
Key Ideas   My Question(s)

Speaker _____   Topic _____
Key Ideas   My Question(s)

Speaker _____   Topic _____
Key Ideas   My Question(s)

Speaker _____   Topic _____
Key Ideas   My Question(s)

Speaker _____   Topic _____
Key Ideas   My Question(s)

What is the role of questioning in testing ideas and theories?

Clarifying the Task

As students work on finding solutions for a problem, or as they near completion of a research project, they will have a variety of possible ideas, theories, and conclusions. Finalizing their decisions is often an onerous task. Sharing and discussing these ideas with a colleague can be very helpful, not only in making final decisions, but also in developing their own personal understanding. In this task, students will be introduced to, and later apply, the consultation process.

Building Understanding

- Discuss the terms "consultant" and "consultation," and how they apply to the business world.
- Ask students to brainstorm the skills and attributes a consultant would require. Chart ideas.

> Skills: active and reflective listening, critical reading, effective questioning
> Attributes: empathetic, encouraging, honest, perceptive
> (Review reflective listening skills if students don't suggest them.)

- Discuss how a businessperson would prepare for meeting with a consultant. Chart ideas.

> - collect and organize relevant data, research notes, and visuals
> - decide on a way to present and share information and ideas
> - rehearse and check to ensure all needed materials are at hand
> - arrange for a quiet meeting space with all the equipment and materials required

- Ask what a consultant would do to prepare for the consultation. Chart ideas.

> - get any available background information on the topic
> - collect and bring note making-materials (laptop, PDI, paper, pens, calendar)
> - arrive prepared to listen, question, reflect, and discuss

Demonstrating Understanding

- ❏ Discuss how students could use the consultation process to help clarify their thoughts on issues, draw conclusions, or decide on solutions for a current curriculum challenge.
- ❏ Provide them with copies of the Consultation to Test Ideas (page 107) and discuss how the consultants can use these question prompts to help them begin. Encourage consultants to develop their own questions based on the specific topic and ideas being tested.
- ❏ Divide the class in to two groups: half will share their research and ideas, the others will act as consultants—listen, question, reflect, and reply.
- ❏ Switch roles and continue the consultation process.

Q Tip
See Working With Information and Testing Ideas, in Koechlin and Zwaan (2001).

Consultation to Test Ideas

Why should I consult with other students about my work?

When you talk about your research or writing with others, you have an opportunity to try out your ideas and reflect on their reactions. Telling others about the information you have gathered and what you have done with it is a sort of thinking out loud. Explaining your ideas to someone else helps you clarify your own thinking. The reactions and questions of another can help you think about your work from different perspectives. This can sometimes help you make new connections or simply confirm your own thoughts. On the other hand, it is also very important for you to stay true to your own analysis and ideas. Consultation is meant to help you clarify your thinking and refine your ideas.

> You understand it only if you can teach it, use it, prove it, explain it, or read between the lines.
>
> (Wiggins and McTighe, *Understanding by Design*)

When is peer consultation valuable?

- Sharing research analysis
- Testing conclusions and solutions
- Making decisions
- Planning a presentation
- Editing your writing
- Preparing a portfolio

Sample Consultation Questions

- What was it about this topic that caught your interest?
- Tell me about your discoveries.
- What did you find that surprised you? disturbed you? gave you pause for thought? tickled your funny bone?
- What is really important about your findings? Why?
- Who or what might this affect? How?
- How did you come to understand...?
- Explain how your thinking about this has changed since you started your research.
- Did you draw any conclusions? find a solution to a problem? make a decision?
- What would you like to see happen now?

Post-Consultation Questions

- Has the conference helped to confirm your thinking?
- How did "thinking out loud" help?
- What changes do you want to make to your work?
- Do you need further advice?
- What are your next steps?

How does a journalist develop interview questions?

Q Task
Students learn to ask questions to glean information through an interview.

Clarifying the Task
Creating effective interview questions is a very difficult task. In this Q Task, students deconstruct the text of an article that was based on an interview, and make inferences to determine the questions the reporter would have asked to obtain specific information.

Building Understanding
- For the purpose of modeling, select an article that has obviously been composed as a result of an interview with a popular athlete or entertainer. Sports and entertainment magazines and web sites provide a rich source. Project it or provide individual copies for students to work from.
- Read the article to the class, asking them to discover something new about the personality.
- Have the students read the article, this time looking for all the information bits revealed by the article. Chart and number the information bits.
- Organize students in small groups to discuss and discover the questions that the reporter might have used to obtain the information revealed in the article. Have groups share their discoveries.
- Discuss the specific merits of suggested questions for each information bit and decide on the best question(s). Record selected questions beside information bits and discuss the features that would have made them successful questions. Identify focus words, and words that facilitate elaboration, clarification, hypothesis, etc.

Demonstrating Understanding
Provide students with copies of a different high-interest article and supply them with highlighters so that they can individually follow the procedure you modeled with them: identifying information bits and creating the questions that might have been use to get the info.
- ❏ Have students use their highlighters to identify the words in the question that they feel will help them glean the information they are targeting. They will record their findings on the Questioning InfoBits organizer (page 109).
- ❏ Have students meet in small groups to share and explain their questioning strategies and select the best question for each info bit. Share selected questions with the class and identify their special features.
- ❏ Discuss how this process will help students be better interviewers. Have them make an entry on in their Reflection Journals or on a Learning Log.

Q Tip
To source high-interest articles, collect current copies of popular magazines and web sites.

Questioning InfoBits

Who is the personality being interviewed?	
InfoBits What are the important bits of information in this article?	**Possible Questions** What might the journalist have asked to get this information?

How do students create effective interview questions?

Q Task

Students learn to create effective questions to use when conducting an interview.

Clarifying the Task

Interacting with people in an interview is a powerful way for students to acquire information firsthand. In this task, students will learn to prepare interview questions. They will follow an interview scaffold and observe questioning etiquette. Students will be expected to respect the fine line between deep, probing questions and invasive, rude questions. In this example, the class is studying career opportunities. They will work in pairs to arrange and conduct interviews with a community member in a field of personal interest to them.

Building Understanding

- As a group, discuss the sort of information students will be looking for. Caution them about the sort of questions that would be taboo.
- Chart their ideas and develop a list of questioning do's and don'ts. See Questioning Etiquette and Guidelines below.
- Discuss the timing of this assignment and the stages of the process:
  - planning the interview
  - creating the interview questions
  - procedures for before, during, and after the interview
  - assessing success

Questioning Etiquette and Guidelines

Good questioners get good results by following some basic guidelines, by being aware of the thoughts and ideas of others, and by just using good manners. To become an effective questioner:
- Listen to the thoughts and ideas of others.
- Don't interrupt others.
- Be mindful of the feelings and the privacy of others.
- Be aware of your own feelings.
- Respect others.
- Show appreciation.
- Stay on topic.

Demonstrating Understanding

The students will have already done research on career roles that they are interested in pursuing. Now they prepare to interview someone currently working in a field they have chosen.

- ❏ Have students make a list of information they hope to glean from the interview.
- ❏ Review tools to help students build effective questions; see chapter 3: Learning to Question.
- ❏ Instruct students to apply their knowledge of questioning strategies and their understanding of the job to create their interview questions.
- ❏ Have students create an interview worksheet listing all their questions with space for recoding interview responses.

Q Tip

To ensure student safety, the teacher may wish to coordinate these interviews with Career Week experiences so that they can be conducted at the school during the school day.

How can students prepare to effectively question an expert?

Clarifying the Task

In this example, the class has been engaged in a study of naturally occurring disasters—earthquakes. They have a good background of vocabulary and knowledge about earthquakes, including how and where they occur. Their study has sparked lots of new questions about the topic, and the teacher has arranged for an Interactive Video Conference (IVC) with a leading seismologist.

Building Understanding

- Contact the expert and discuss the content you want students to gain from the IVC experience. Plan the structure of the IVC with the expert.
- Provide students with background information about the work of a seismologist, or instruct students to research and share their knowledge of careers related to the study of natural disasters.
- Provide students with the Expert Planning organizer (page 112). Have students develop a web or concept map of what they already know.
- Review question building tools such as the Question Builder Chart (page 65), Question Builder Frames (page 68), and Question Stretchers (page 79). Provide students with copies so they can experiment with building effective questions to ask the seismologist.
- Have students record their best questions on the Expert Planning organizer.
- Have students share their questions in groups. Each group will cluster similar questions and decide on three questions the group would really like to ask. Ask each group to chart their questions.
- Examine all the questions, looking for similarities, and cluster questions. Discuss the questions with the class and decide on six really important questions everyone wants to have answered.

Demonstrating Understanding

- ❏ Arrange for students to take turns practising how they would ask the six important class questions. Inform students that they need to be prepared to ask any of the six class questions plus one of their own, as time permits during the IVC lesson.
- ❏ Provide students with any IVC technical information they need, such as being prepared for a time delay between audio and visual play. Remind students of best manners for hosting a guest.
- ❏ Have students keep notes on their Expert Planning organizer during the conference.
- ❏ After the conference they can record any further questions they have and plan to research their new inquiries.

Expert Planning

Topic: _____   Date: _____

What do you already know about this topic? Build a web to show what you know.

What do you want to find out?	What did you learn from the expert?
Build questions you would like to ask the expert. Pick your best question.	

Do you have more questions now?	Where can you look for answers?

How can primary students create survey questions?

Q Task

Students will work as a group to create questions for a survey.

- Who are we going to survey?
- What is that we need to find out from our survey?
- What is a healthy breakfast?
- What are the things people might eat?
- What might they drink?
- What if they don't eat and drink healthy foods?
- How can we phrase the questions to get one-word or list answers?

Clarifying the Task

Designing and conducting a survey is a powerful way for students to acquire primary information on a topic; it is sometimes the only method of acquiring current data. It is a big challenge to create specifically focused survey questions that will garner the information needed in the form of easily usable data. In this Q Task, the teacher will lead the students through the process of creating survey questions and a survey form for students to use. In this example, the class has been studying personal nutrition. The final activity will be to collect information from students in the school to determine how healthy their breakfast eating habits are. This will be done through a survey.

Building Understanding

- Collect some simple survey samples and show students how surveys are set up. Explain that the questions must be carefully crafted in order for them to find out what they need to know. Guide student thinking and together generate well-focused survey questions.
- Once you have identified all the information you require to determine if breakfast habits are healthy, begin to compile a set of questions to get this information. Encourage students to anticipate answers and think about what those answers mean for their questions. Test them within the class to see how well they work as survey questions. Rephrase questions where necessary. Discuss how to record the answers to the questions; e.g., checklist, short answer, multiple choice. Talk about how to deal with the answers not on their checklists, and any other concerns the students have. Review rules of etiquette.
- Produce a survey questionnaire and a recording form. Make enough copies so that each student can survey three or four others. Arrange with other teachers to have students available to be surveyed.

Demonstrating Understanding

- ❏ Have students practise the survey with a learning buddy.
- ❏ Students should read the survey questions and record each answer on the form.
- ❏ Remind students to thank those surveyed for participating, and explain that the results will be shared (posted on the school web site or a bulletin board, announced over the PA, covered in a newsletter, etc.)
- ❏ Collect all the survey results. Collate and tabulate the answers from the survey in a visual format.
- ❏ Examine the findings and look for patterns. Encourage students to react to their findings. Ask students how well the questions worked, and what they would change for next time.

Q Tip

For more information on creating surveys, see Koechlin and Zwaan (2003).

How can questions enable comparison?

Q Task

Students will use their questioning skills to make comparisons.

Clarifying the Task

In this example, the class is beginning a study of plants and animals. They will formulate questions they have about the needs of plants and animals, and look for similarities and differences.

Building Understanding

- Introduce the concept of needs by reading a story about a newborn baby and discussing the needs of babies. Chart student responses. What do babies need to stay healthy?
- Set up a Jigsaw learning experience.

Task 1: Research Groups	Task 2: Expert Groups
Develop questions that will help you investigate the needs of plants/animals.	Compare your questions in new groups.
Group A Forest Animals	Group ABCD
Group B Farm Animals	Group ABCD
Group C Trees	Group ABCD
Group D Vegetables	Group ABCD
Provide each group with sticky notes and lots of non-fiction books about their focus topic. Have students individually browse through the books and record their questions on sticky notes. Share and add more/new questions on their stickies	Provide students with chart paper. Ask them to sort their question stickies, look for similarities, and cluster similar questions about the needs of plants and animals. Students name question clusters to identify categories: survival, water, habitat, etc.

Debrief with the class and create a T-chart.

Questions we have about the needs of plants and animals

	Similar	Different
Survival		
Habitat		
etc.		

Demonstrating Understanding

Each student will select three questions they want to explore, and prepare for research using the Exploring with Questions organizer (page 115).

Q Tip

See further models for working with information in Loertscher, Koechlin, and Zwaan (2005).

Exploring with Questions

Questions	Plants	Animals	Where I found my information
1)			
2)			
3)			

How do students know which attributes to compare?

Q Task
Students will question the aspects of items to establish criteria for comparison.

Clarifying the Task

Making comparisons is a complex task. Students must first understand exactly what is being compared and why they are making the comparison. In early comparing experiences, the teacher will provide the criteria, but ultimately the students will do it themselves. In this task, students practise discovering the comparison criteria.

Building Understanding

- Introduce to students the need to establish criteria on which to base a comparison. Explain the need to look carefully at the items to be compared and to make individual determinations for each different case.
- Model an example comparing bicycles. As extensive background knowledge of the items to be compared is essential, collect ads from flyers and catalogues to use as reference materials for details about different kinds of bikes.
- Have students ask questions about the features or aspects of bicycles using a projection or a chalkboard version of the Comparison Criteria organizer (page 117). Look at the list of aspects and select any that are appropriate for your comparison.
- Emphasize that the words on the list are only suggestions. Students can extrapolate, bend, twist, or spin the words to find the nuance that fits their need. For example, in comparing bicycles, the important factors might be price, size, weight, material, model, and features, such as gears and tires. Have students think again about bicycles to identify additional characteristics.
- Have students consider why they are making the comparison, as it may help them identify important criteria. Add these to the list.
- Have students look carefully at the attributes selected and select four criteria that are most important for their purpose. Students need to be prepared to explain the rationale for their selections.

Demonstrating Understanding

- ❑ Create small groups and give each group an item for which to identify criteria; e.g., sports equipment, animals, schools, games, TV shows, communities, vacation destinations, etc.
- ❑ Provide groups with copies of the Comparison Criteria organizer (page 117) to guide their questioning as they identify criteria.
- ❑ Remind students that this questioning will help them identify aspects to compare, but they may want to use terms more suitable to their purpose; for example, if they are comparing tennis courts to decide which club to join, the criteria might be price/fee, location/transportation, structure/court surface, and programs/coaching (the rationale for selecting "coaching" as a criterion could be that they are hoping to enter competitions and want an extra edge).
- ❑ Once they have established important criteria and identified those to be used for the comparison, have students work individually to complete the What's the Same? What's Different? organizer (page 118).

Q Tip
This strategy can be applied to comparing poems, plays, characters in a novel, etc.

Comparison Criteria

I will be comparing _____

because _____.

What is important to me is _____

_____.

Potential Comparison Criteria

Are there aspects related to

- ❑ size, number?
- ❑ color, mood?
- ❑ price?
- ❑ texture, material?
- ❑ use, purpose, intent?
- ❑ needs, food, equipment?
- ❑ programs, courses?
- ❑ structure, organization?
- ❑ special features, adaptations, options?

- ❑ taste, flavor?
- ❑ safety features?
- ❑ stability, duration, longevity?
- ❑ style, form, model?
- ❑ components, sections, departments?
- ❑ attractions, characteristics?
- ❑ shape, design, format?
- ❑ location, environment, habitat?
- ❑ odor, aroma, scent?

Important criteria for this comparison.

_____   _____

_____   _____

_____   _____

_____   _____

Now circle the four criteria you will use for your comparison.

What's the Same? What's Different?

Topic:

Topic:

Comparison Criteria and Rationale	What's different?	What's the same?	What's different?
Criteria: Why?			
Criteria: Why?			
Criteria: Why?			

Adapted from Koechlin and Zwaan (1997)

What role do questions play in building understanding?

Q Task

Students will apply their questioning skills to help them develop understanding of unfamiliar text.

Clarifying the Task

In this Q Task students will use their questioning skills to build understanding when they read. This approach can be used with picture books, non-fiction books, textbook chapters, and articles.

Building Understanding

- Review the question starters: *who, what, when, where, why,* and *how.*
- Select an engaging picture book related to your topic of study.
- Look at the cover and have students ask questions about the cover. Chart the questions, highlighting the question starters.
- Read a few pages and have students make up more questions. Continue charting and questioning until the book is completed.
- Ask students: Are there any questions that we now have the answers to? How could we find answers to some of your other questions? How have questions helped us to enjoy the story more?

Demonstrating Understanding

❏ Provide groups of three or four students with a text for read-aloud sharing, or multiple texts on the same topic for independent reading. This strategy works well with both fiction and non-fiction texts.

❏ Have students practise the strategy using the Question, Question organizer (page 120). They will record their questions before reading, during reading, and after reading the text.

❏ Have students circle or highlight the question starters they have used. Remind them to make use of all the question starters if they can.

❏ Ask students to review their questions and cross off all the ones they now have answers to.

❏ Have students share in their group and see if anyone else has the same or similar questions about the topic. They could use a coding system to mark questions already answered, similar questions, and different or unique questions.

Q Tip

Students could follow this task by identifying a question or several questions they are really curious about and begin a new quest to discover the answers.

Question, Question

I am reading _____

by _____

How do questions help me when I read?

Before Reading

During Reading

After Reading

☑ I know the answer now.	★ No one else has this question.
☺ Someone has the same question.	◉ I am really curious about this.

Adapted from Loertscher, Koechlin, and Zwaan (2004)

How can students use FAQs to demonstrate or share their learning?

Q Task
Students will share their learning by creating Frequently Asked Questions and Answers.

Clarifying the Task

In this example, senior students are developing online orientation presentations to help students and parents new to their school. They will work in groups, each group taking responsibility for a department in the school. One component of each presentation will be Frequently Asked Questions and Answers.

Building Understanding

- Collect examples of pamphlets, posters, and web sites that provide information about an organization, location, or service. Set up the samples in stations and have the students rotate through the stations so they examine as many exemplars as possible. Have them discuss in their groups the samples that seem to be the most effective, and why.

- When students have had time to examine and discuss a number of samples, instruct them to work in their groups to establish criteria for an effective information presentation.

- Discuss with the class the purpose of the frequently asked questions and determine how one decides what questions to include; e.g., predicting the needs of the client, little-known information, highlighting key services, etc.

Demonstrating Understanding

- ❏ Students will work in groups to gather needed data about the department they have been assigned. They will need visuals, such as video footage, digital photos, and graphics.
- ❏ Once they have their raw data, they need to think like the student or parent new to the school and develop a set of FAQs.

School Library Information Centre FAQs

- What kinds of resources are in the library?
- How do I find what I need?
- How can I get help for projects?
- Can I use the photocopier?
- When can I use the computers?
- Can I access any resources and help from home?
- What happens when I lose a book?

- ❏ Once students have worked out the visual support for their presentation, the questions, and the answers, have them consult with another team to discuss their plans and confirm that they have thought of all the needs of new students and parents. See the Consultation to Test Ideas organizer (page 107).
- ❏ Presentations can be created in a slideshow format and mounted on the school web site for new students and parents to access.

Q Tip
This strategy can easily be applied to any content subject; e.g., ecosystems, eating disorders, the Gulf War, etc.

How can peer questioning enhance student creative writing?

Q Task

Students will develop questions to help peers revise or extend their writing.

Clarifying the Task

Revision is a critical component of the writing process; however, self-criticism is a difficult concept. In this Q Task, students will learn how peer questioning helps to improve their writing. The focus is on the content rather than the grammar. In this example, students have been listening to and reading a generous selection of mystery stories and novels. They have identified the common elements of the mystery genre and are now ready to apply this knowledge to their own writing.

Building Understanding

- When students have written and edited their first draft, ask them to find a partner to conference with. Instruct them to read their mystery stories to their partners and then exchange stories.
- Have each student fold a piece of paper in half and write statements of praise on one half and questions they have about his or her partner's story on the other.

Great!	Questions
Your title really caught my attention.	How could you improve your title so it doesn't give so much away?

Demonstrating Understanding

Students will read the praises and questions about their story and reflect on any possible revisions they may want to make. Reassure students that their own original ideas are most important, but their partner's questions will be indicators of areas where further clarification may be needed to make their writing the best it can be.

Q Tip

Just as professional writers credit their editors and those who made contributions to the revision process, ask your students to credit the partner who contributed to revisions with probing questions.

How can we use Book Talking Strategy?

Clarifying the Task

This strategy provides an engaging alternative to traditional book talks.

Building Understanding

- Select four or five novels with a common theme, author, or genre. Read the novels and select an interesting passage from each that will capture the students' interest and spark curiosity and probing questions. Practise reading each selection so you are prepared to model good read-aloud techniques; e.g., intonation, pacing, body language, etc. Introduce each novel before reading the chosen passage.
- Provide students with a few minutes to think about the passage, then instruct them to formulate and share questions they have about the novel based on the reading you provided. Take four or five questions from the class, and chart them if time allows.
- Continue with the next passage until all the books you selected have been introduced.

Watch your copies of these books disappear at checkout time!

Demonstrating Understanding

Design a book-report activity following the same format. When students have finished reading their novels, instruct them to select an engaging passage from the text and practise reading it aloud to the class as you have modeled. The rest of the class will ask questions based on the passage read. This time the reader will answer the questions. Watch more books disappear at checkout time.

Q Tip

The passages and questions can be displayed to attract browsing readers. The display could be located in the library or on the library web site.

5. Questioning to Progress

How does self-questioning help students assess their efforts and the connection to actual results?

Ultimately we want students to take responsibility for their own learning, so throughout the learning process we need to build in opportunities for reflection. Students reflect on their effort, the process they pursue, and their learning in terms of skills, attitudes, and knowledge: thinking about resources and strategies they used, thinking about what they have learned and what they need or want to learn next. The success of these reflections is to a large extent based on their ability to apply effective questioning.

Marzano, Pickering, and Polluck (2001) tell us that reinforcing effort and providing recognition is a strategy for increasing student achievement. These researchers make us aware that most children do not readily see the link between the effort put forth in an assignment or task and the quality of the results, although it may seem painfully obvious to us. The good news is they can learn to make the connection.

In this chapter we will share a few tools to cultivate student thinking about learning. We have paid special attention to trying to capture the essence of self-questioning to assess their effort and the connection to actual results.

- How can self-questioning help students manage time and resources?
- How can students create a quiz for a test review?
- How can I teach the SQ4R study strategy?
- How do students know which resource is the best for their needs?
- Q Task Quickies: Questioning to Progress

> Questioning is central to learning, changing and growing.
> (Jamie McKenzie, *Learning to Question to Wonder to Learn*)

How can self-questioning help students manage time and resources?

Clarifying the Task

Parents and teachers often take on all the responsibility for monitoring the completion of student homework and assignments. What we want is to move towards developing self-reliance in our students. In this task, students will learn how self-questioning will help them be more successful by saving them time and anxiety.

Building Understanding

- Read "Grasshopper Logic" from *Squids will be Squids* by Jon Scieszka, or another story or humorous poem to introduce the topic of homework. Invite the class to share personal homework stories.
- Remind your students that busy people need to ask themselves questions to keep organized and to ensure that they remember everything. Share with students your self-questioning process for making sure you have everything you need before you leave school to go home for the evening.

- What time is the next bus?
- How long can I work on marking before I have to leave the school?
- Do I have all the essays for grading?
- What else did I want to work on tonight?

- Have students work with a partner and brainstorm questions to ask themselves that would help them do a better job with their homework. Ask each group to share a couple of their ask-myself questions.

Demonstrating Understanding

Provide students with copies of a blank Game Board template (page 126). Ask students to select some of the ask-myself questions and to create more questions of their own that would really help them win at homework.

Sample questions:

- Did I record my homework as soon as it was assigned?
- Am I sure I understand the homework?
- Did I ask the teacher for help with what I don't understand?
- Do I have the phone number of my learning partner so I can get help if I need it?
- Do I have a quiet place to work?
- Do I avoid distractions from television and phone calls?
- Have I planned an early homework time so I'm not too tired?
- Have I planned to takes breaks when I need them?
- Are my notebooks, paper, pens and pencils, etc. organized?
- Did I put all my homework together by the door to take to school?
- Did I get all my assignments in on time?

Game Board

Ask yourself good
questions and Win the
Homework Game

Homework Check Bookmarks

Homework Check ✔

Subject 1 _____

What must I do? _____

_____

Which books do I need?

_____

_____

What other materials do I need?

_____

Where can I get help if I need it?

_____

_____

Subject 2 _____

What must I do? _____

_____

Which books do I need?

_____

_____

What other materials do I need?

_____

Where can I get help if I need it?

_____

_____

Subject 3 _____

What must I do? _____

_____

Which books do I need?

_____

_____

What other materials do I need?

_____

Where can I get help if I need it?

_____

_____

Homework Check ✔

Subject 1 _____

What must I do? _____

_____

Which books do I need?

_____

_____

What other materials do I need?

_____

Where can I get help if I need it?

_____

_____

Subject 2 _____

What must I do? _____

_____

Which books do I need?

_____

_____

What other materials do I need?

_____

Where can I get help if I need it?

_____

_____

Subject 3 _____

What must I do? _____

_____

Which books do I need?

_____

_____

What other materials do I need?

_____

Where can I get help if I need it?

_____

_____

How can students create a quiz for a test review?

Q Task

Students create a quiz to review content material when preparing for a test.

- What is the main idea?
- Why is this important?
- Who is it important to?

Q Tip

As a more active strategy, create consultation lines—pairs of chairs facing each other: one side questions; the other answers. The members of each group number off: even-number students make up the question lines; odd-number students, the answer lines. Then switch lines so that everyone has a chance to ask and answer. Rotate through the lines, so that different teams face off against each other.

Clarifying the Task

In this Q Task, students will apply questioning skills and tools to study for exams in content areas such science, history, literature, and geography. (See chapter 3: Learning to Question.)

Building Understanding

Review questioning strategies learned in the 20 Questions Task (chapter 1, page 17), riddle activities (chapter 1, pages 20–23), and the Question Builder Chart (chapter 3, page 65). Use a topic-related picture book, a short textbook selection, or an article to model the process.

- Read to identify the main idea(s) of the piece and why it merits study.
- As a group, create questions that students could ask study partners to test their understanding of the topic. Record questions on a chart.
- Read the text again, this time focusing on the details that support the findings from these questions: sequencing of events, connections and relationships, causes and effects, impacts, turning points, implications, etc.
- Have students work in small groups to create questions that will elicit this information. Remind students that, while dates and numbers are important, we also want to test understanding of the topic, so they must include questions that go beyond simple recall of details.
- Share and record the questions with the whole class. Discuss the merits of their questions and identify areas of importance that might have been overlooked. Cluster questions by question starter. Work together to build a chart detailing how the question starter gives directions to the answer they are looking for.

Q Chart

Question	Answer
What	facts, one-word answers, lists, etc.
Where	location, destination, etc.
When	date, time, etc.
Who	partners, stakeholders, victims, participants, etc.
How	methods, instructions, process, etc.
Why	reasons, cause and effect, etc.
Which	decisions, problem solving, prioritizing, etc.

Demonstrating Understanding

❏ Have students work in small groups to develop quiz questions, using content material that will be tested in the near future. Remind students to use the Q Chart to ensure that they are developing a good variety of questions.

❏ Meet with groups as they complete their quizzes and provide feedback for refining them.

❏ Have students produce a working copy of the quiz for each team member.

❏ Jigsaw the groups (regroup) to answer the quizzes.

How can I teach the SQ4R study strategy?

Clarifying the Task

This cross-curricular strategy can be used effectively to introduce new text or to prepare for tests. Students will apply their questioning skills to help them understand a new text or review curriculum content.

Building Understanding

- Model the process with students, using a selected text related to your topic of study, such as an article, a chapter in a content text, or a web site. Provide students with your overall guiding question or a statement of purpose for studying this particular text.
- Introduce the SQ4R Process Steps (below) and go through each step with a think-aloud, so students experience a working model of the approach to reading and clarifying text.

SQ4R Process Steps

1. **S**urvey: Quickly skim the text making use of features that give an overview: headings, subheadings, visuals, specialized text, hyperlinks, etc.
2. **Q**uestion: Jot down several questions that come to mind about the text as you skim.
3. **R**ead: Read the material strategically to find the answers to your questions. Keep track of new questions you have as you proceed.
4. **R**ecite: Close the text. Share your discoveries with a study buddy, using your questions to guide your discussion. Phrase your personal responses in your own words. Refer back to the text to confirm ideas whenever discrepancies arise.
5. **R**ecord: Make a record of your new understanding of the text. Use the SQ4R Study organizer (page 130) or design your own.
6. **R**eview: Review your questions and notes. Did you find the answers to all your questions? If not where can you find information to help you?

Demonstrating Understanding

❏ Provide students with a new text related to your topic of study. Provide the SQ4R Study organizer (page 130).
❏ Instruct students to apply the strategy and complete the organizer.
❏ Debrief to consolidate content learning. Ask students to make an entry in their Learning Log, reflecting and assessing the SQ4R process.

Q Tip

One of the oldest study systems, SQ4R (Survey, Question, Read, Reflect, Recite, Review) teaches students to attack a text and monitor comprehension in a series of sequential steps. (Robinson, 1970)

SQ4R Study

Name _____

Text _____

I am studying this text because ...

My Questions	Answers from the Text
1)	
2)	
3)	
4)	
5)	

New Questions and Next Steps

☐ Survey
☐ Question
☐ Read
☐ Recite
☐ Record
☐ Review

How do students know which resource is the best for their needs?

Clarifying the Task

Info-glut is a major problem for young researchers. Determining whether or not resources are useful and reliable sources of information is a critical step when dealing with volumes of data. In this Q Task, students will learn how good questions help them decide if a resource will be useful for their purpose. In this example, students are preparing to investigate the structure and function of local, regional, and national government bodies.

Building Understanding

- Discuss why careful analysis of resources for this task is important. Provide small student groups with a variety of non-fiction resources to support this topic: non-fiction books, magazines, pamphlets, videos, and Internet sites.
- Ask students to explore the resources and determine how to find out if these resources will be good for their investigations. Where do you look for evidence that this is a good reliable source? Chart student responses: skim for readability, find copyright date, read the review/synopsis on the back cover, determine author's credibility, etc.
- Debrief and add criteria the students may have missed—credibility, accuracy, intent, context, and perspective.
- Provide students with copies of the Examine and Evaluate Resources organizer (page 132) Using the question prompts on the organizer, do a think-aloud modeling of how to evaluate several different kinds of resources. Model by reviewing several resources that are not good sources, such as a web site developed by a special-interest group or an old text with out-of-date information about government.
- Discuss further the importance of evaluating resources and how helpful guiding questions are in this process.

Demonstrating Understanding

- ❏ Instruct students to evaluate a print resource and a web resource they are considering for their research. Have them use the Examine and Evaluate Resources organizer (page 132). After completing the organizer, students should be able to make an accurate decision about the usefulness of the resource.
- ❏ When students have had lots of practice, have them develop their own questions for judging the suitability of books, Internet sites, videos, etc. Ultimately this process will become intuitive.

Q Tip
Provide students with clues for analyzing the anatomy of a URL address.

Government sites	**.gov**
Education	**.edu**
Commercial sites	**.com**
Non-profit organizations	**.org**
Military	**.mil**
Countries	**.us**, **.ca**, **.au**, etc.

Examine and Evaluate Resources

Title _____

Author _____

Publisher _____

What is your research question? What kind of information do you need?	
Validation Criteria	**Notes**
Accuracy • Up to date • Statistical data/facts • Opinions	
Authority How credible is the writer/producer? • Qualifications • Experience Who financed the work? • Corporation • Government agency • Special-interest group	
Perspective Whose perspective is included? Whose voice is excluded?	
Slant/Intent What is the purpose? • Inform • Convince/Promote • Entertain • Question • Support	
Context What is the context of the piece? • Historical • Political • Environmental • Social • Fiction • Factual	
Evidence of Bias • Exaggeration • Prejudice • Inclusion/exclusion • Charged words • Overgeneralization • Opinion asserted as fact	

> **Bottom Line**
>
> Will this resource be useful for your project?
>
> Why? Why not?

Questioning to Process

Assessment Tools

Give students some ownership of the assessment process. Ask students to brainstorm the criteria they feel are key to assessing a presentation, such as an oral report or a multimedia presentation. Agree on the general criteria and have students work in groups to develop questions; e.g., Did the presenter communicate with the audience? Collate the questions and prepare a rating scale or checklist to assess presentations.

QUERY

At the culmination of a project or assignment, discuss with students the power of self-assessment. Model for students the questions you would ask yourself as you assess the results of a project, such as an event you organized for the school. Give students copies of the QUERY to Self-Evaluate organizer (page 134); discuss the acronym and the criteria it represents. Provide students with lots of time to reflect on their learning process and develop self-analysis questions. They do not have to record their answers to these questions, but must be prepared to discuss them in their assessment conference.

Mirror, Mirror

When students can articulate what they were supposed to do on a task and honestly reflect on how well they did to meet the learning objectives, they are learning how to progress—how to move forward and improve their results. Have students fold a piece of paper in half. On the lefthand side they answer the question, *What was I supposed to do?* Opposite, they answer, *How did I do?* Now have students set goals for next time.

Reflective Questions

Students will benefit from recording their questions, as well as their thoughts and feelings, after a learning experience. Use organizers such as the Learning Log (page 135), or have students start or finish their response journals with a question they are pondering.

Please Help

Invite your students to pose a question they want you to answer about the quality of their work, such as *How can I put more suspense in this short story?* or *I have solved this problem but I wonder if there is a shorter way.*

QUERY to Self-Evaluate

Q Question yourself to determine your task success quotient. Develop three questions for each of the QUERY criteria to help you measure your performance with a task or project.

U Understanding of skills and new knowledge

Q 1

Q 2

Q 3

E Effort and efficiency

Q 1

Q 2

Q 3

R Results of process and product

Q 1

Q 2

Q 3

Y Yens for next time

Q 1

Q 2

Q 3

★ Be honest with yourself.

★ Celebrate your success.

★ Target your weak points for improvement.

Learning Log

Date:		
Activity:		
Thoughts	Questions	Next Time

Date:		
Activity:		
Thoughts	Questions	Next Time

Date:		
Activity:		
Thoughts	Questions	Next Time

6. Moving Forward

Where do we go from here?

This is not the end. We hope this book will be the beginning of a questioning journey for students, teachers, and schools. We have shared our practical experiences; these strategies have worked for us. We hope our readers will now be inspired to select strategy ideas, adjust them to suit their particular needs, and try them out with students. In this section we have developed some suggestions and strategies for moving forward with questioning.

☑ **Build a bank of organizers and templates**

To help your students keep their questioning strategies at their fingertips, we suggest that you keep blank templates for questioning in a readily accessible portfolio, just as you keep samples of graphic organizers and other writing templates for students to use as they need them.

☑ **Model the question building process.**

We have developed two process charts that may help students remember and apply steps to creating good questions: Steps to Building Good Questions (page 137) and Question Tips for Students (page 138). These tools will help students develop thinking processes for building effective questions. Use these charts to model the development of questions for research projects. Ensure that students "own" the question; engagement and effort will be guaranteed.

☑ **Infuse questioning in the design of units and assignments.**

Make use of the flow chart How Do We Nurture the Process of Inquiry (page 8) when you are designing inquiry tasks.

☑ **Develop teacher questions to frame learning experiences.**

Use some of the questioning strategies from chapter 3: Learning to Question as you develop overarching questions to focus units of study or information tasks. Start with curriculum standards. Decide what the essential learnings are and create a big idea question to frame the learning experience (Wiggins and McTighe, 1998).

☑ **Learn more about the role of questioning in learning.**

Consult References list (page 140) for further resources that will help as you continue to build a questioning repertoire for students. Start a folder of professional support material.

☑ **Take Action.**

Now take time to develop your action plan. Complete the Next-Steps Teacher Planning Map (page 139).

Steps to Building Good Questions

◇**?** What is the purpose of your question?

- ❏ fact finding
- ❏ connecting to reading
- ❏ focusing research
- ❏ probing for meaning
- ❏ making a decision
- ❏ solving a problem
- ❏ evaluating resources
- ❏ making comparisons
- ❏ studying for a test
- ❏ creating/inventing something
- ❏ analyzing your progress
- ❏ setting new goals
- ❏ other _____

◇**?** Who will your question help?

- ❏ me
- ❏ my classmates
- ❏ my team
- ❏ my family
- ❏ my community
- ❏ other _____

◇**?** Where can you look for answers to your question(s)?

- ❏ thinking about my own experiences
- ❏ asking an expert
- ❏ conducting a survey
- ❏ using reference materials
- ❏ researching several resources
- ❏ other _____

◇**?** Experiment with some of the question builder templates. Create lots and lots of questions.

◇**?** Review and revise your question to meet your information need.

◇**?** **Pick your best and proceed with your inquiry.**

NOTE: You may need to revise your question(s) again as you proceed with your research.

Question Builder Templates

- I Wonder Wheel
- Question Builder Chart
- Question Builder Frame
- Six Thinking Hats
- Power Up Q Cards
- Power Up Your Inquiry Question
- Question Stretchers
- Building Questions and Focus Statements with Bloom

Question Tips for Students

Start by thinking about your answer.

Why do I need this information?
- What is it that I need to know?
- What will I do with this information?
- Is it just for me, or will I be sharing my learning with others?

Is the information readily available?
- Can I find it on my own?
- Do I need help?
- Who would be the best person to help me?

Where might I find this information?
- Can I make a phone call?
- Do I need to search in information resources?
- Will I need to do a survey, poll, or interview?

How do you build the right question? By asking more questions!

"Can I find what I need by asking a simple question using who, what, where, when?"
   e.g., What is the telephone number of the video store? Where is the video store located?
If YES, compose and pose your question. If NO, continue.

Will the answer require some explanation?
If YES, ask, "Should I begin my question with How or Why?"
   e.g., How can I get to the video store? Why isn't the video store open 24/7?

Is my information need more complicated? Do I need a question that focuses on a specific aspect of the topic?
If YES, use **focus** words, such as *change, job, purpose, value, function, capacity, intent, type, role, structure, lifestyle, defence, survival, result, outcome, kinds, importance, characteristics, relationships, adaptations, conditions, infer, imply,* etc.
   e.g., How has the function of video store changed since the invention of DVDs?

Do I need more in-depth data? Should my question prompt analysis?
If YES, use **relationship** words, such as *significance, consequence, project, implication, connection, correlation, pattern, trend, compare, contrast, cause, effect, value, analyze,* etc.
   e.g., What has caused the significant drop in rentals at the video store?

Now ask, "Will the question I have created get me the information I need?"

Is it too broad? Will it get me more than I need or want?
   Or
Is it too narrow or too shallow?

Take a last look at your question and revise it if necessary.

Pose your question and begin your quest for the answer.

Next-Steps Teacher Planning Map

Where does questioning logically fit in curriculum?

How will I start to build a comfortable questioning environment?

Which questioning skills and strategies will I teach first?

How can I keep track of my students' questioning progress?

How can I empower students to take ownership of questioning to learn?

How can I promote the idea of the Student as Questioner with my students, school, and community?

Resources

References and Selected Resources

Abilock, Debbie (2004) "Information Literacy From Prehistory to K–20: A New Definition" *Knowledge Quest AASL*, March–April. http://www.ala.org/ala/aasl/aaslpubsandjournals/kqweb/kqarchives/vol32/32n4abilock.pdf

Barell, John (2003) *Developing More Curious Minds*. Alexandria, VA: Association for Curriculum Supervision and Development.

Bloom, B. S. (1956) *Taxonomy of Educational Objectives, Handbook I: The Cognitive Domain*. New York, NY: David McKay Co Inc.

Booth, Wayne C. (2003) *The Craft of Research*. Chicago, IL: University of Chicago Press.

Cecil, Nancy Lee (1995) *The Art of Inquiry: Questioning Strategies for K–6 Classrooms*. Winnipeg, MB: Peguis Publishers.

Ciardiello, Angelo V. (1998) "Did you ask a good question today? Alternative cognitive and metacognitive strategies" *Journal of Adolescent & Adult Literacy*, 42 (3), pages 210–20.

Carrier, Roch (1984) *The Hockey Sweater*. Montreal QC: Tundra Books.

Christian, Peggy (2000) *If You Find a Rock*. New York, NY: Harcourt, Inc.

de Bono, E. (1985) *Six Thinking Hats*. Boston, MA: Little, Brown, and Co.

Gonsalves, Rob (2005) *Imagine a Day*. New York, NY: Simon and Shuster.

Gonsalves, Rob (2003) *Imagine a Night*. New York, NY: Simon and Shuster.

Green, Judy. (1999) *The Ultimate Guide to Classroom Publishing*. Markam, ON: Pembroke Publishers.

Harvey, Stephanie and Goudvis, Anne (2000). *Strategies that Work*. Portland, ME : Stenhouse.

Koechlin, Carol and Zwaan, Sandi (2005) *Ban those Bird Units: 15 models for teaching and learning in information-rich and technology-rich environments*. Salt Lake City, UT: Hi Willow Research and Publishing.

Koechlin, Carol and Zwaan, Sandi (2003) *Build Your Own Information Literate School*. Salt Lake City, UT: Hi Willow Research and Publishing.

Koechlin, Carol and Zwaan, Sandi (1997) *Information Power Pack: Junior and Intermediate*. Markham, ON: Pembroke Publishers.

Koechlin, Carol and Zwaan, Sandi (2001) *Info Tasks for Successful Learning*. Markham, ON: Pembroke Publishers.

Koechlin, Carol and Zwaan, Sandi (1997) *Teaching Tools for the Information Age*. Markham, ON: Pembroke Publishers.

Lundy, Kathleen Gould (2004) *What do I do about the kid who…?* Markham, ON: Pembroke Publishers.

Manzo, A.V. (1969) "The ReQuest Procedure" *Journal of Reading*. 13 (2), pages 123–6.

Marzano, Robert J., Pickering, Debra J., and Polluck, Jane E. (2001) *Classroom Instruction that Works*. Alexandria, VA: Association for Curriculum Supervision and Development.

Marzano, Robert (2005) *Building Background Knowledge for Academic Achievement*. Alexandria, VA: Association for Curriculum Supervision and Development.

McKenzie, Jamie (2005) *Learning to Question to Wonder to Learn*. Bellingham, WA: FNO Press.

Morgan, Norah and Saxton, Juliana (1994). *Asking Better Questions*. Markham, ON: Pembroke Publishers.

Ogle, Donna M. (1986) "K-W-L: A teaching model that develops active reading of expository text" *Reading Teacher*, 39, pages 564–70.

Postman, Neil and Weingartner, Charles (1969) *Teaching as a Subversive Activity*. New York, NY: Dell.

Robinson, F. P. (1970) *Effective Study(5th ed.)*. New York, NY: Harper & Row.

Scieszka, Jon (1998) *Squids will be Squids*. New York, NY: Viking.

Thomas, Lyn (2001) *Ha Ha Ha*. Toronto, ON: Maple Tree Press.

Weiderhold, Chuck (1995) *Cooperative Learning and Higher Level Thinking*. San Juan Capistrano, CA: Kagan Cooperative Learning.

Wiggins, Grant and McTighe, Jay (1998) *Understanding by Design*. Alexandria,VA: Association for Curriculum Supervision and Development.

Willems, Mo (2004) *The Pigeon Finds a Hot Dog*. New York, NY: Hyperion Books for Children.

Wilson, Janet (2000) *Imagine That*! Toronto, ON: Stoddart Kids.

Wolfe, Patricia, (2001) *Brain Matters*. Alexandria,VA: Association for Curriculum Supervision and Development

Videos

Baked Alaska (2003) Videocassette/DVD. London, UK: Stanner Films Ltd and Journeyman Pictures. 26 min

Pit Pony (1997) Videocassette. Halifax, NS: Cochran Entertainment. 92 min

Chandler's Mill (1990) Videocassette. Dramatic Canadian History Series. Toronto, ON: National Film Board of Canada. 30 min.

Web Sites

Bloom's Taxonomy's Model Questions and Key Words
http://www.utexas.edu/student/utlc/handouts/1414.html

Framing Essential Questions
http://www.fno.org/sept96/questions.html

Q Matrix Products
http://www.kaganonline.com/Catalog/index.html

The Question is the Answer
http://www.fno.org/oct97/question.html

Question Matrix
http://sci.tamucc.edu/~eyoung/4382/question_matrix.html

Questioning.org
http://questioning.org/

Questioning Techniques for Gifted Students
http://www.nexus.edu.au/teachstud/gat/painter.htm

A Questioning Toolkit
http://www.fno.org/nov97/toolkit.html

Index